suburban space

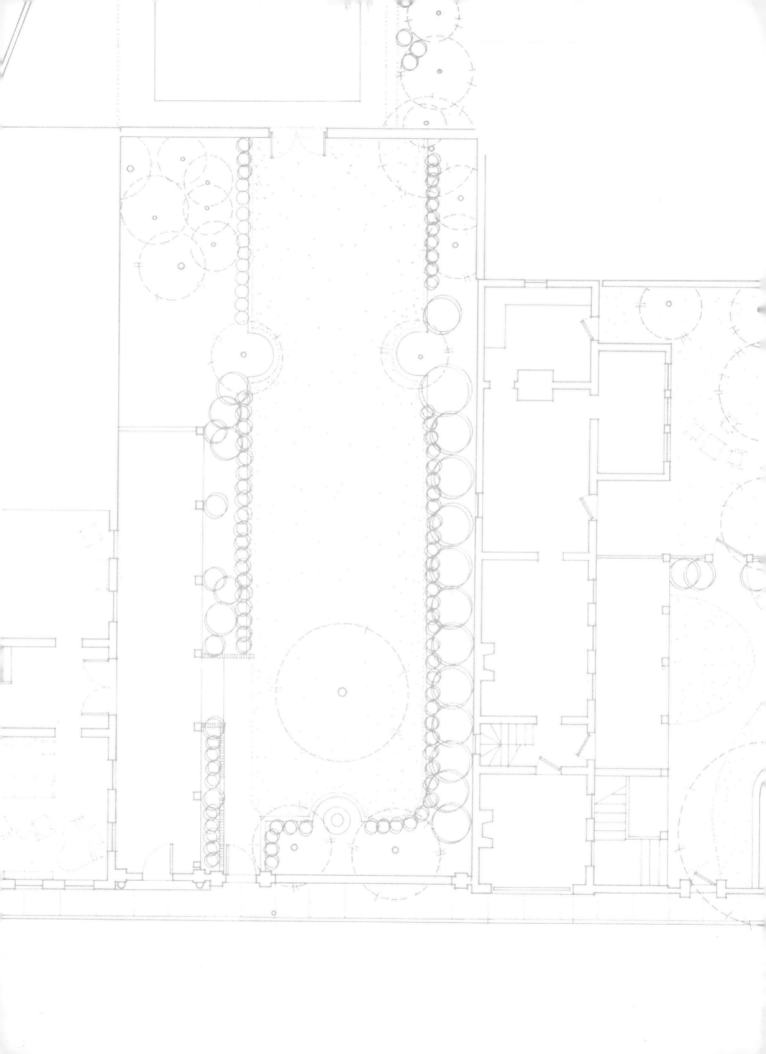

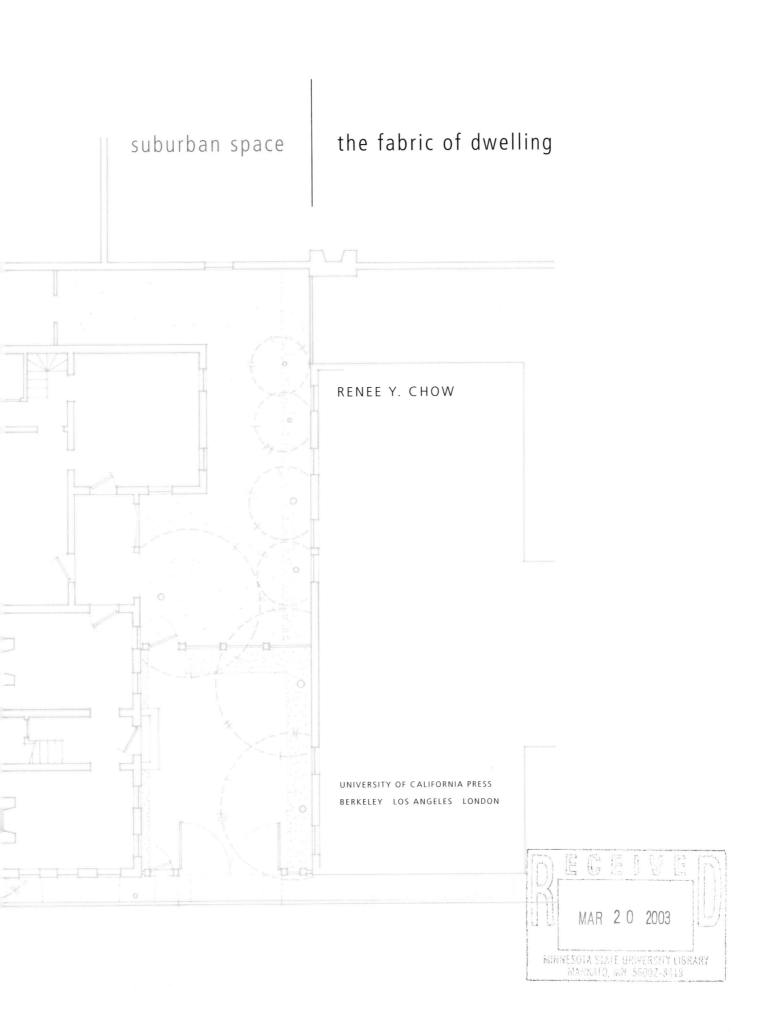

suburban space | the fabric of dwelling

RENEE Y. CHOW

UNIVERSITY OF CALIFORNIA PRESS

BERKELEY   LOS ANGELES   LONDON

The following chapters appeared previously in different form in the following publications and are published here by courtesy of the respective publishers: chapter 4 as "Representing Detached Dwelling: A Survey," *Journal of Architectural Planning and Research* (Summer 2002); chapter 5 as "House Form and Choice," *Traditional Dwellings and Settlements Review* 9 (1998): 51–61; chapter 6 as "Sharing in a Setting," *Places* 11 (1997): 64–65; and chapter 8 as "Designing Density," *Transformations of Urban Form*, edited by Gian L. Maffei (Firenze: Alinea Editrice, 1999).

University of California Press
Berkeley and Los Angeles, California

University of California Press, Ltd.
London, England

Library of Congress Cataloging-in-Publication Data
Chow, Renee Y., 1955–.
    Suburban space: the fabric of dwelling / Renee Y. Chow.
        p.   cm.
    Includes bibliographical references and index.
    ISBN 0-520-23386-7 (alk. paper)
    1. Suburbs.   2. Housing development.   3. Housing, Single family.
4. Dwellings—Design and construction.   I. Title.
HT351 .C49   2002
307.74—dc21   2001052278

Manufactured in the United States of America

11   10   09   08   07   06   05   04   03   02

10   9   8   7   6   5   4   3   2   1

To TC and our girls

contents

illustrations

illustrations

acknowledgments

Ten years ago, four students and I went knocking on the doors of houses in Cambridgeport, interrupting people we had never met to ask if we could measure and draw every room in their houses. Then we asked to go outside and do the same. Little did I know that our discoveries about households and their settings would lead to this book on the suburbs. The research on which this book is based is the work of many, and I am grateful to those who have guided, helped, and encouraged me in so many ways.

The seeds for this research were planted in my days at the Massachusetts Institute of Technology. From my teachers and, later, my colleagues, a framework for my study of architecture was built. Theoretical underpinnings, learning through observing, methods and representations, and the practice of architecture as a "fabric" are constructs that I developed with the faculty at MIT, especially N. John Habraken, Maurice K. Smith, Jan Wampler, Shun Kanda, and Imre Halasz. Their insights into and disciplined views of the physical environment were instrumental in shaping mine.

For the fieldwork in this book, I am indebted to many, many people. First and foremost, I would like to acknowledge the residents who greeted my students, my research assistants, and me with great openness, and even coffee and cookies. Without their willingness to let us into their personal world, this book could not have been written. Shun Kanda introduced me to Rudolf Schindler and Irving Gill in 1980, sending Tom Hille and me to Los Angeles in 1980 to research Pueblo Ribera, the Laurelwood Apartments, and the Sachs Apartments, as well as Horatio West Court. Since then, I've been back to knock on those doors two more times.

Students in my seminars and classes at both MIT and the University of California, Berkeley, have taught me about the breadth of ways of living. In particular, I would like to acknowledge the clear thinking of Swati Chattopadhyay, my teaching assistant in the first year I taught "Housing American Cultures." Also, Cynthia Wardell introduced her classmates

Ann Edminster, George Guu, Elena Rinaldi, Mike Ma, and Maria Vrdoljak to all her neighbors in San Francisco. For joining me in a very long one-day field trip to Radburn in the fall of 1992, I'd also like to acknowledge the fieldwork of Lilian Sung, Angela Barreda, Sid Bowen, Daniel Gorini, Julie Kim, Kari Kimura, Albert Kong, Neil Harrigan, Shuh-Hwa Sih, and Rodrigo Vargas.

Research assistance was a catalyst when the work seemed too overwhelming for one. Antje Steinmuller helped with the survey work in Charleston in 2001 and with meticulous observations for other case studies. In 1996, Gen Urban helped me survey houses in San Francisco. Connie Cagampang Heller worked with the three-dimensional modeling of both Levittown and the Sachs Apartments in 1994. Julie Kim helped reconstruct our field notes from that crazy day at Radburn in 1993. And Helen Jeffries did initial reconnaissance in 1990, wandering through both Levittown and Radburn in the winter cold. The funds for this research assistance came from the Humanities Arts and Social Sciences Fund at MIT and the Committee on Research and the American Cultures Program at U.C. Berkeley.

The Radburn Homeowners Association supported the research and sent a letter of introduction to the home owners of the four cul-de-sacs we visited in 1992. For the south Charleston case study, E. E. Fava, architect, in Charleston, graciously provided drawings of a house that he is renovating.

Three people provided encouragement to keep writing at crucial times. Anne Vernez Moudon kept reminding me that I was writing two books, one graphic and one verbal, so I should expect to take more time. Nancy Ruttenberg, with her great sense of humor, lent her time to edit and review my prospectus—keeping me laughing when I was too serious. And Charlene Woodcock, the architecture editor at the University of California Press, has been supportive and key in prompting me to hit deadlines just when I was ready to relax.

Prior to bringing this research together as a book, I wrote several articles that served as the basis for several chapters in this book. Chapter 4, "Seeing Suburban Dwelling as a Fabric," is an expanded and revised version of "Representing Detached Dwelling: A Survey," which appeared in the *Journal of Architectural Planning and Research* (Summer 2002). Chapter 5, "Accommodating Choice," is based on "House Form and Choice," which appeared in *Traditional Dwellings and Settlements Review* 9 (1998): 51–61. The seeds for chapter 6, "Sharing in a Setting," were planted in *Places* 11 (1997): 64–65.

The observations and concepts in this book are the result of collaboration with Thomas Chastain, my partner, husband, and fellow explorer of fabrics of dwelling. We began our research about people and their settings some twenty years ago in Turfan, and from China to Europe and throughout the U.S. he has inspired, directed, and questioned our research as well as surveyed many of the case studies with me. It is through his encouragement and insistence that I wrote this book. Chapter 8, "Designing Density," is based on a studio that we taught together and an article (also entitled "Designing Density") that we coauthored for *Transformations of Urban Form*, edited by Gian L. Maffei (Firenze: Alinea Editrice, 1999). But every chapter is as much his as my own.

introduction

MAKING A NEIGHBORHOOD BY AGGREGATING INDIVIDUAL HOUSES IS SEEMINGLY STRAIGHTFORWARD and simple. This deceptive simplicity lulls the design professions, policy makers, and, ultimately, suburban dwellers into an inattentive acceptance of a house-by-house development of the residential landscape. And while concerns for the social and environmental consequences of suburban development are intensified by the consistently large numbers of annual single-family housing starts,[1] there are surprisingly few alternatives proposed for this kind of housing. With the exception of a few practices,[2] the architectural profession largely has been eliminated from suburban housing design. Today, with suburban design subsumed by marketing and with a culture of architects increasingly uninterested in the mundane everyday, the architectural profession either has been thwarted or has withdrawn from the suburban housing debate.

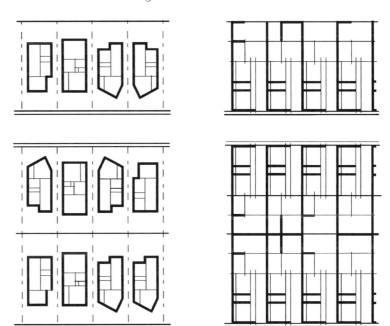

1. Two paradigms of detached housing.

Although we pretend that suburban houses are independent from one another, they are in fact interrelated, and their interrelationship needs to be acknowledged and designed. This book describes how seeing the suburbs as a fabric—a continuous structure of spaces in which we reside and through which we move and look—allows designers to describe relations not just within but among houses. When the suburbs are seen as a fabric, the attributes for which they have been criticized—lack of community, homogeneity, and the waste of land and resources—can be reevaluated as the consequences of accepting an overly simple aggregation of discrete and independently structured masses. When the concept of "dwelling" is reconceived as an interdependent weaving of individual and collective ways of dwelling, an alternative framework emerges for the design of detached dwellings. With a weaving of a fabric for dwelling—a weaving of people to places, houses to setting, indoors to outdoors—the discipline of architecture is reinserted into the suburban housing debate.

observing dwelling

The motivating questions behind this research arose some twenty years ago when I chanced upon Rudolf M. Schindler's Sachs Apartments in the Silver Lake district of Los Angeles. This residential setting held the distinctive presence of each resident, of a neighborhood, and of the architect. What is the relationship among residents as individuals, their physical and collective context, and the role of the designer? These apartments led to a quest to understand how the phenomenon of dwelling is formally cultivated and sustained and to compare neighborhoods in Boston, Charleston, San Francisco, Levittown, and Radburn and housing complexes designed by Schindler and Irving Gill, as well as residential settings less renowned but with lessons equally important to this study.

In this book, the term *suburb* is used as shorthand to describe neighborhoods of single-family detached houses. Although the term also is used to describe geographic positions outside city centers or relatively low-density built environments, a physical definition of settings of detached houses has been essential for the work of this book. To learn about the suburbs and their potential, case studies were needed that looked beyond the conventional suburban subdivisions and their problems to fabrics that have been successfully inhabited through successive generations. Given this simple definition of settings of detached houses, case studies could be found in city centers, outlying metropolitan areas, and rural settings.

The basis for this alternative view of neighborhoods was a simple curiosity to observe and describe how we live in our suburbs; I did not wish to make generalizations but rather sought to see the particular ways we conduct our day-to-day lives. I wanted to understand the potential of the physical setting to support or limit everyday choices.

This book explores ways of describing the character of communities through the ways in which individuals dwell. It flows from a fundamental assumption that the activities of dwelling have the potential to take place everywhere in the built environment. That is to say, we experience and use our built environment as a continuous structure of spaces and elements that we dwell in, move through, and look upon. This view of the environment, commonly referred to as a fabric, is prevalent in urban studies and in disciplines such as sociology, geography, and urban morphology that examine settings in which buildings are attached.[3] It is also found in studies of traditional architecture that emphasize the interaction of everyday activities and habits with the form of settlement.[4] Therefore, although the concept of the built environment as a fabric is well established, its theories and descriptions have not been extended to single-family detached housing environments. The approach presented in this book emerges from these various disciplines, tempered by directing the research toward informing design.

One of the first tasks of the research was to describe the suburbs as a fabric—what should be observed, and how should it be represented? The work of several people contributed to the development of my own technique for representation. Saverio Muratori (figure 2) and Klaus Herdeg provided the initial constructs for rendering the continuity of the physical structure of fabrics.[5] Rather than using more traditional, hierarchic representations of the suburbs, the documentation in this book is presented at one scale to capture the experience of being within a fabric.[6]

2. Plan of Venice that captures the experience of being in a fabric: "Tav. II—Quartiere di S. Zulian—Situazione Attuale," by Saverio Muratori.

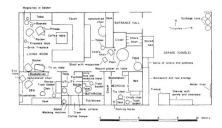

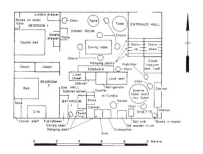

3. Plan that captures one household's dialogue between house form and choice: "The Bottom Level of the Johnson House" and "The Top Level of the Johnson House," by Susan Kent.

But we do more than exist in the spaces of our fabrics. In the conduct of our everyday activities, we inhabit a fabric—positioning artifacts to use, to remind, to control, and to personalize our space. Observations of spatial patterning by cultural anthropologists such as Susan Kent (figure 3)[7] and vernacular studies conducted by architects and historians[8] provided a technique to relate cultural activities to spatial form through the study of the artifacts of dwelling. The kinds and positions of furniture and other personal belongings are mapped on to plans and sections that present a picture of dwelling as a dialogue between ways and places of living.

Therefore, representing a fabric requires drawing houses on contiguous lots with both interior and exterior spaces rendered both as they are built and as they are actually inhabited. The drawing (whether in plan or section) needs to emphasize the quality of dwelling as it is experienced—from room to room, house to yard, house to house, and house to street.

Another task of the research was to collect such representations of suburban settings for comparative study. A survey of literature revealed little documentation of American suburbs as inhabited. Robert L. Vickery's St. Louis study documented the inhabitation of one neighborhood, but only the areas outside of the houses.[9] Horacio Caminos's "dwelling group" documentation represented both interior and exterior spaces, but the inhabitation was shown in only one house.[10] As a result, it was necessary to conduct my own fieldwork (a sample of which is shown in figure 4). In each location, a combination of field measurements, photography, and informal interviews was completed. In the process of surveying houses, it became clear that the lack of previous studies did not reflect the value of the information but the difficulty of gaining access to people's homes.

As I assembled the body of documented settings, I made comparisons to define and test attributes that described detached housing as a fabric. As a result of this process, I defined my criteria for case study selections: repeating patterns in the residential settings, which enabled me to study both differences and similarities in use and the effects of time; adjoining lots, enabling me to study house-to-house relations; and varying identification of cultural groups, enabling me to compare residents' choices. The differences and similarities in habitation, house form, and setting expose how the formal structure of a setting is critical for supporting dwelling.

Parallel to the documentation of suburban ways of living was the development of graphic means to describe the dynamics between how people dwell and where they dwell. Since this research was ultimately directed toward informing design, any analysis useful to understanding dwelling relations also needed to be useful in directing the design process. In designing a fabric, representations need to be contingent, allowing designers to put forth sketches that reveal possible solutions or that can be integrated with other issues in consideration.[11] The work of

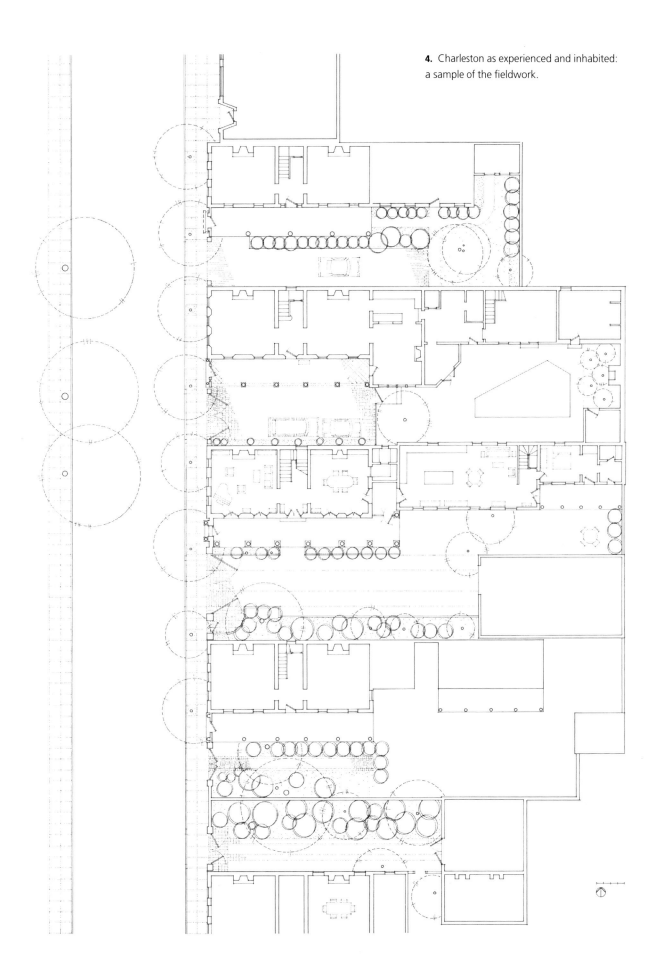

4. Charleston as experienced and inhabited:
a sample of the fieldwork.

several urban and housing theorists proved helpful: N. John Habraken's territorial structuring of urban environments; Bill Hillier's analysis of access at the urban level; Richard C. MacCormac's analysis of dimensional zones in the work of Frank Lloyd Wright; and Stanford Anderson's overlays describing public and private claims in the streets of Paris (see examples of their work in figures 5–8).[12]

5. "Sub-Variations in the Twin Support System" (Habraken et al. 1976).

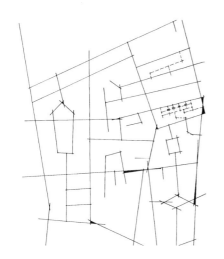

6. Axial map of Barnsbury (Hillier and Hanson 1984).

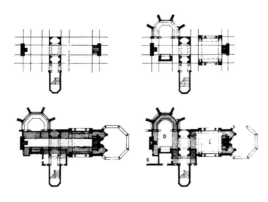

7. "The Exterior of the Husser House," designed by Frank Lloyd Wright; drawing by Richard C. MacCormac.

8. "Area of Avenue Victor-Hugo. Engineering Structure," by Stanford Anderson.

All use systemic overlays that bridge the hierarchic, inside-outside, building-by-building distinctions that cause breaks in seeing and designing the continuous quality of dwelling. These methods of observing places share two premises regarding people and the environment. The first is that the relationship between people and the built environment over time can be analyzed through the study of physical form. The second is that form, while not deterministic, is critical to behavior and use.

To explore relations within a fabric, I used a range of attributes drawn from both architectural design and planning. These attributes, described in chapter 4, include *dimensions*, or the sizes of spaces for inhabitation; *access*, or how people move through a setting; *claim*, or how they establish control over a space; *assemblage*, or how the form of the house is built; and *containment*, or the organization of privacy.

When the descriptions and design of these attributes moved from a house-by-house to a house-to-house approach, two kinds of suburban settings emerged—volumetric and fabric. In a *volumetric* setting, critical relations occur at the shells of houses in a majority of the attributes studied. Dimensions change between inside and out: access coherently laid out within a home is disconnected from its exterior surroundings; privacy is reinforced at the perimeter of the house. A majority of postwar and contemporary suburban housing is volumetric (figures 9a and 9b).

9a, b. Detached houses in a volumetric setting.

10a, b. Detached houses in a fabric.

In a *fabric* setting, some or all of the attributes extend beyond a single house and are shared among houses (figures 10a and 10b).

In other words, an attribute is not just ordered at the house level but organizes the house with its setting as well. Through the use of overlays, the contrast between the discontinuity of volumetric settings and the continuity of fabrics is immediately apparent. Seeing the systemic qualities of a larger landscape for dwelling makes possible the design of rooms, houses, streets, and yards as integrated and equal parts of a fabric. This approach looks beyond the imagery of neighborhood and the simple positioning of volumes of houses to see how environments are structured to support dwelling. Observing the attributes of dwelling as systems enables clearer description of the architectural component of suburban criticism—how the form of housing amplifies concerns about uniformity, isolation, and lack of sustainability.

What follows should be seen not as a method for designing housing but as a critical framework intended to change how the suburbs promote dwelling. This book intentionally avoids prescribing ways to design suburbs, since there is no universal method that is particular enough to encompass the diversity of people, places, and practices. Seeing and designing single-family detached dwellings as a fabric is a critical position that equally values the uses of inside and outside spaces. It values each locale as a unique social and physical setting in which the collective setting is made by individual contributions. It is a framework that supports the potential to stay within a community rather than move when ways of living change, and it sees dwelling as both connected and secluded—so that public and private are seen not as oppositional but as reciprocal.

Professional practice has segmented design of communities into the house, the yard, the street, and the city, each to be designed by its own specialist: the architect, the landscape architect, the transportation planner, the urban planner. As each profession focuses on its own solutions, gaps in design emerge that isolate house from yard, yard from street, and neighbor from neighbor. But the activities of dwelling move across these professional domains. If the criticisms of suburban waste, isolation, and intransigence are not founded in the single-family house but in a compositional paradigm of sites as bounded objects, the design professions must find ways to collaborate. This book argues for a look at housing from a perspective based on knowledge shared by the environmental design professions—an alternative view of single-family detached housing that supports diverse choices of ways to live, that provides desired private outdoor space but does not waste it, and that allows opportunities for individuals and households to build their own sense of community, one that can change over time. This book is for anyone, whether designer, developer, administrator, or resident, who is concerned with the cultural and environmental viability of the suburbs.

part one | seeing the suburbs as a fabric

THE FIRST PART OF THIS BOOK QUESTIONS HABITS AND PROPENSITIES TO SEE AND DESIGN HOUSING as bounded sites—to make us aware of our tendencies to see the single-family house as distinct and separate from its setting. This part, comprising four chapters, introduces a way to see housing as a fabric and proposes ways to observe and represent relations among detached buildings.

The first chapter, "Beginnings of a Production System," introduces two ways to see detached housing: as a continuous and interdependent weaving of individual homes or as a discontinuous and discrete placement of private houses. The end of World War II brought a profound transformation of the ways in which single-family housing was conceived and produced. With the return of U.S. veterans, Americans embarked on an unprecedented course of private residential construction. Despite the variety of spatial models for affordable housing design already available, a mass-produced, volumetric approach was advanced by developers and financed by government institutions, and it came to influence broadly the social, economic, and political landscape. The book's second chapter, "Persistence of the Box," reviews the consequences of this approach and argues that the problems identified in criticism of suburbia—its isolation, commodification, and waste—are symptoms of a volumetric conception of the single-family house. The chapter considers why past criticism has been ineffective in changing these "little boxes" (as Malvina Reynolds's folk song, made popular by Pete Seeger, termed them) and their resulting patterns of sprawl. Chapter 3, "Defining Dwelling," lays out alternative assumptions for the design of detached houses. It offers a view of dwelling as an exchange, or dialogue, that brings together where we live and how we live, each informing and changing the other. Chapter 4, "Seeing Suburban Dwelling as a Fabric," evaluates traditional methods of representing suburbs and the consequences of these tools of depiction for the form of suburbs. Additional means of representation are introduced, based upon a systemic rendering of the continuities and discontinuities in a setting.

| beginnings of a production system

BUILT LANDSCAPES THAT FLOURISH AND ENDURE ARE RICH AND COMPLEX, MANIFESTING THE CHOICES of residents and visitors alike. We admire these settings for the multitude of ways they support being in a place—in the city, in the neighborhood, in the street, in the room. These environments connect us to their places through a continuity of spaces, without distinct boundaries between buildings, between inside and outside, or between public and private, and without absolute separation between plots of ownership.

The design and building of these continuities are necessary competencies too often ignored. The complexity, choices, and changes inherent in the settings for residential life are difficult to describe, and in attempts to clarify the relations for design, the tendency is to simplify. The suburban, single-family detached residential setting serves as a case in point. In the division of work into manageable design tasks, suburban design focuses on house, street, and lot subdivision. This promotes dwelling in insular, self-contained, bounded spaces with minimal connection, permeability, and openness. The potential of a setting as a fabric is lost, and what remains is more a collection of objects than a landscape—yet we live in the landscape.

The possibilities for connection and continuity in the suburbs are enormous. There are overlaps and extensions between gardens and rooms, retaining walls and house walls, individual and shared territories, extended views and near views, permeability and containment. When settings are configured, structured, and assembled so that each individual action is seen as contributing to the field of the place, freestanding houses are never seen as detached. The subject of suburban space is not the house or yard, neighborhood or region, each discrete and independent of the others. Rather, it is the continuities and the possibilities for dwelling.

As a general rule, the propensity to see objects foregrounds the house as the subject in the suburbs. To see the field—the relationships and

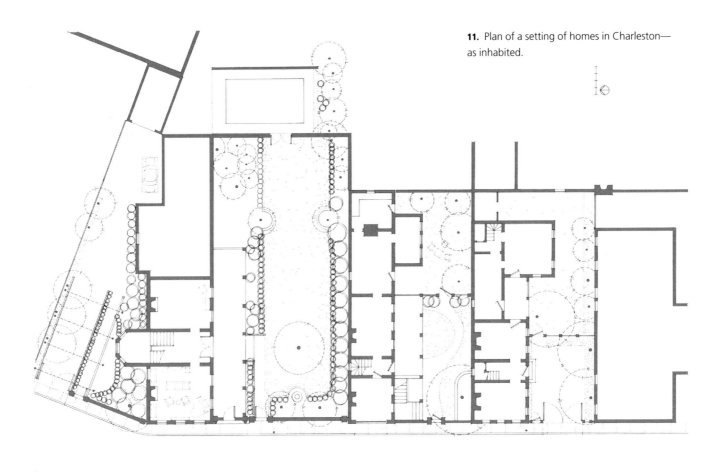

11. Plan of a setting of homes in Charleston—as inhabited.

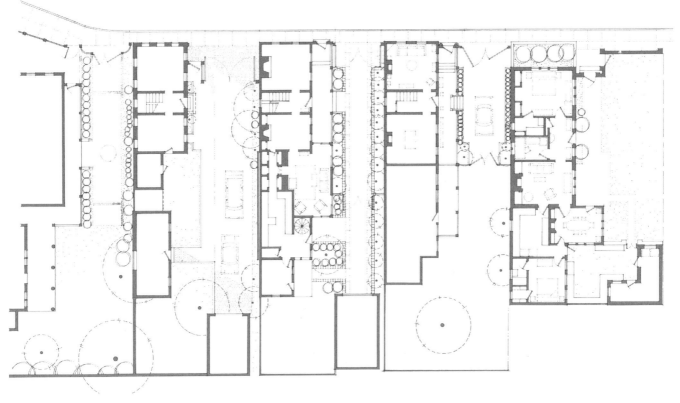

continuities between sites and activities—requires an intentional shift in focus. In the shift, fabrics for dwelling are highlighted and revealed as commonplace in urban, suburban, and rural landscapes. Some continuities are accidental, and the shared structuring emerges only through habitation and over time. Others are embedded intentionally, as part of the design.

fabrics for dwelling

12a, b, c. Charleston.

CHARLESTON, SOUTH CAROLINA Renowned for its houses and gardens, Charleston has a unique fabric of detached housing. The houses— long, rectangular, freestanding structures—are organized perpendicular to the street (figure 11). Typically, the gable end of each house faces the street (figure 12a), and the house's rooms are organized along a wall on a northern or eastern lot line. Porches, locally known as *piazzas*, and side yards parallel the depth of the houses on the south or west side (figure 12b). A solid door controls access from the street to the piazza. When open, the door provides visual access into the piazza, extending the public realm. When closed, it protects the porch from direct public view, extending the private space of the house into the side yard.

The side yard is a lush, green garden that accommodates parked cars as well as paths to a garage deeper in the lot. The side garden is formed by a piazza to the north and by a wall of an adjoining neighbor's house to the south that provides welcome shade from the summer sun. Between the street and the side yard, a screened gate or fence gives the passing pedestrian a view into the garden (figure 12c).

Each level of a typical house has two rooms, one in front and one in back, separated by a stair. The south side of the rooms is oriented toward the side yard for both light and view. The north wall of the house is solid, without any windows, and each room has a fireplace centered on this wall. Deeper into the lot, the houses extend on a room-by-room basis, still maintaining southern orientation toward the side yard and northern separation.

A description of the Charleston house must include the side yard, just as a description of the side yard requires inclusion of the two bordering houses. It is this interdependent structuring of detached houses that characterizes the pattern of dwelling as a fabric. The fabric is built by alternating indoor and outdoor rooms that are defined by shared walls and connecting piazzas. The walls maintain the autonomy and privacy of each household, forming a seam shared by adjacent neighbors as well as providing a collective structure for the larger neighborhood. The piazza connects house to side yard, extending the realm of one into the other. Whether inside or outside, in the public or household domain, one senses the texture of shared and overlapped spaces. As one walks along

13. Plan of the Horatio West Court Apartments—as inhabited.

most Charleston streets, the alternation of houses and gardens gives one the impression of being in both a densely built neighborhood and an extended garden.

14a, b, c. The Horatio West Court Apartments.

THE HORATIO WEST COURT APARTMENTS Unlike Charleston, where individual houses are assembled to form a setting, Irving Gill's Horatio West complex of four apartments,[1] in Santa Monica, California, illustrates the weaving of a collective fabric in which detached residences can be found (figure 13). This court complex is organized around a common path, simultaneously pedestrian and vehicular, that runs perpendicular to the street, passing through the entire depth of the lot to reach garages at the rear of the site (figure 14a). Moving along this path, one is flanked first by low garden walls, then by terraced landings that lead into arched entries (figure 14b). Continuing deeper into the site, one moves into a bright courtyard with grass on either side of the path, again passing another pair of terraced landings and arched entries (figure 14c). Directly ahead, an arched gateway spans the path. Passing under the archway leads one to the parking courtyard, flooded with sunshine, where the pavement widens for the navigation of cars.

What is not immediately apparent is the form of the individual houses. It is difficult to recognize where one house ends and the next house begins. Instead, components of the fabric—for instance, steps and terraces, high and low garden walls, entry halls, and volumes of rooms—are read as defining both the individual houses and the complex. The boundaries of the four houses become apparent only within each house.

As in Charleston, indoor and outdoor spaces contribute equally to the fabric. The outdoor patio spaces, contained within high garden walls, extend the spaces of the adjoining interior rooms, making both indoor and outdoor spaces seem larger. The center lawns both separate the front and rear houses and form a shared courtyard. Together, the lawns and patio walls of all four houses form the space of the largest courtyard. In this way, every space of the site is valued, both inside and out.

QUADRUPLE BLOCK PLAN In the early 1900s, Frank Lloyd Wright was engaged in the "destruction of the box."[2] At many levels—room, house, and site—Wright was changing the form of dwelling, from dwellings characterized by spaces defined at their perimeter by four walls and a ceiling to dwellings characterized by spatial overlap and connection. Wright transformed the nature of dwelling by de-emphasizing the room-by-room and house-by-house enclosure of space and suggesting instead a weaving and interpenetration of spaces that supported connections and continuity— from activity to activity, between inside and out, from room to room, from neighbor to neighbor, and from house to setting.

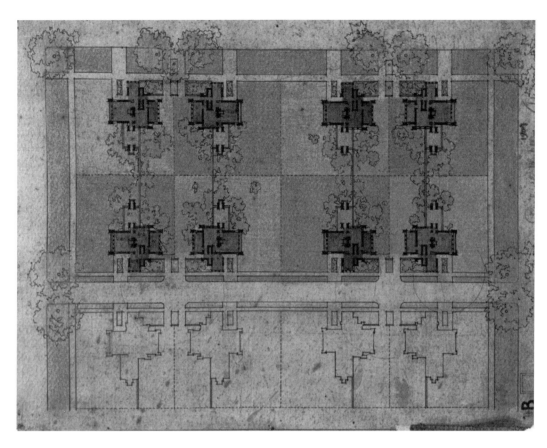

15. Quadruple block plan, by Frank Lloyd Wright.

Unlike his later designs for Usonian houses and the decentralized community of Broadacre City, Wright's early work focused on an intentional interdependence between detached houses. In a series of projects, all entitled "Quadruple Block Plan,"[3] he explored the building of detached houses that are spatially connected without compromising privacy. The project shown in figure 15 is for Oak Park, Illinois, and was designed in 1903. About a 1901 version published in the *Ladies' Home Journal*, Wright wrote: "The block plan . . . shows an arrangement of the four houses that secure [*sic*] breadth and prospect to the community as a whole and absolute privacy both as regards each to the community, and each to each of the four."[4]

As Gill did with Horatio West, Wright developed a basic layout of houses in quadrants in which he explored the various ways that the spaces of detached houses could be interrelated through both house and landscape components. Unlike the closed and containing forms of Horatio West, the orientation of the elements of Wright's houses produced outward-looking, diagonal views to the horizon of the larger setting from the interior spaces of the houses while protecting against the loss of privacy across side yards. As in Charleston, privacy was not controlled by walls at the outer perimeter of the house but embedded in the overall structuring of the houses in their setting.

In this weaving, Wright explored a fabric's potential to hold choices of association among neighbors. In his sketches, Wright projected potential scenarios of habitation, exploring relations between households in one cluster as well as with adjoining clusters. The front entry path of one house could be read as paired with a neighbor's at their shared lot line. Each household then determined the degree of interaction with its neighbor at the entry. If shared, the two paths could be read as one zone of entry; if individual, the paths could be read as separated, divided by the strip of planting that over time the residents might let grow quite tall. Other associations were also possible—across the street, across rear yards, and across side yards. Like the entry paths, these associations were collective if residents chose to share the spaces, but adding garages or landscaping would privatize and separate the households. Over time, each resident or group of residents could determine the nature of their associations, intentionally or informally. This potential for choices in sharing could not be achieved solely by designing the house or the outdoor space. Only by designing the setting as a fabric could diverse ways of sharing evolve.

Wright's early plans for the quadruple block were never realized, and in the mid-1930s, he advanced another version of the quadruple plan, this time as part of an ideal plan for a community that he called Broadacre City. In his comprehensive vision for decentralized living, the houses of the block plan were dispersed onto square, 1-acre lots, increasing the size of the lots to six times that of the original plan.[5] This dispersal diluted the potential associations between neighbors, as well as the economic feasibility of the original scheme, contributing to critiques of Wright's work as a progenitor of modern suburban sprawl. In subsequent discussions of Broadacre City as either utopian or impractical, the significance of the quadruple block plan as a fabric is lost.

volumetric approaches to suburban space

When seen in morphological terms, detached housing could be described as being on a continuum from a setting characterized by interwoven continuities, thus a *fabric*, to a setting of discrete, cell-like *volumes* characterized by discontinuities. In fabrics, attributes of dwelling have continuous or shared spatial relations—reinforcing connections between inside and out as well as from house to house. Individual houses are related in such a way that each contributes to the building of a cohesive physical and social landscape. The other, volumetric end of the continuum is characterized by boundaries and discrete, objectlike houses. Thus, the privacy of a household is controlled at the outer walls of each house. Houses are identified by their exterior shells that separate inside from out, guarding the private from the public. Every setting contains both some degree of continuity and discontinuity, but volumetric settings are more distinctly isolated and discrete.

RADBURN One renowned example of housing design at the volumetric end of the continuum is Radburn, in Fairlawn, New Jersey. Laid out in 1928 by the planners Clarence Stein and Henry Wright, Radburn was intended to showcase the concept of a garden city in America. Though only partially completed due to the bankruptcy of the development corporation, Radburn has been championed as a model for building communities in green, landscaped settings.

The basic components of the Radburn approach are superblocks, community parks and facilities, vehicular networks, and pedestrian paths. The superblock is a large parcel of land surrounded by clusters of houses (figure 16). Pedestrian paths wind through the elongated, recreational greens within the superblocks (figures 17a and 17b), and a hierarchic system of arterial, collector, and service cul-de-sacs defines the outer boundaries of the superblocks. Vehicular roads and pedestrian paths run independently of each other.[6] At the time of Radburn's construction, automobiles were just becoming commonplace, so the walkways were assumed to be the principal way for residents to reach the town center to shop or to catch a train to work. Therefore, houses were oriented so that living spaces and main entries faced the walkways that led to the greenbelts. The kitchens, seen as part of the servicing of the household, were adjacent to the automobile cul-de-sacs (figure 17c).

A volumetric approach was key to arranging the plan. From its conception, the houses were seen as masses placed in a careful composition so that their outer shells shaped the components of the community plan. Thus, the cul-de-sacs were defined by the placement of the houses. Houses were placed close together at the neck of the cul-de-sac to form an entry from the road, and they were spread out at the other end of the cul-de-sac, providing space for a vehicular turnaround

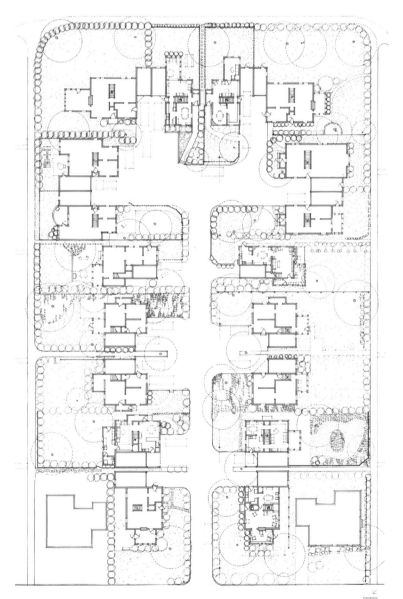

16. Plan of a cul-de-sac at Radburn—as inhabited.

17a, b, c. *Above left:* Radburn (Fairlawn, New Jersey).

18. *Above right:* Radburn—"Plan of Residential Districts Dated November 1929," by Clarence Stein.

and lining the parks with houses. These clusters then ringed the superblocks, defining the parks (figure 18).

Today, the community of Radburn thrives, although not entirely as envisioned by its planners. The dominance of the car as primary means of transport changed the use of the walkways to recreational. This reversal of primary access, from walking to driving, eventually led residents of each household to reorient their way of living in the house to match the reality of their arrival and departure. What was once the "front" yard, adjoining the walkway, is now the "back."[7] Living rooms look out onto private back yards. Front entry porches have been converted into rooms or enclosed as back porches. Side vestibules are now the main entries. Lined with kitchens and eating areas, the cul-de-sac is no longer seen as a service area but as the common space for a group of neighbors. Landscaping, holiday decorations, and children abound in this common court in which drive, walk, paved patios, and gardens are all intermingled. Despite small houses and traffic congestion, residents choose to stay in Radburn for the "neighbors."[8]

at a crossroads

While not offered as ideals, the above examples together illustrate a small portion of a much larger debate about ways that detached housing supports the connection of people to place and about the economics for achieving more housing. Radburn was an effort at economy in infrastructure and house cost as well as an exercise in planning and landscape design.[9] Horatio West was part of an extended practice by Gill to design "social housing for low-income groups."[10] All were proposed or built prior to World War II.

Between 1945 and 1946, 10 million American men and women were discharged from the armed forces; they returned to re-establish families, to find jobs, and to face a dire shortage of housing. This shortage did not come as a surprise. The National Housing Agency estimated that the country would need at least 5 million new housing units immediately after World War II and 12.5 million units in the following decade. The government anticipated this demand, preparing a financial plan, a transportation infrastructure, and housing standards that were biased toward the development of single-family detached houses outside city centers. The veterans' mortgage guarantee program ensured home ownership by enabling veterans to borrow the entire appraised value of a house with no down payment. To qualify for a loan, houses had to be inspected to see if they met Federal Housing Administration (FHA) standards. This process favored new house construction based on model homes because approval of a new house plan automatically extended to all standardized models of the same plan. Older homes needed to be inspected on a case-by-case basis. The cheapest available land for mass housing was almost by definition land at the periphery of cities, and highway funding ensured that the new suburban home owners could commute to jobs in urban centers.

With a forecasted need for millions of units of housing and a government predisposed toward single-family detached housing outside city centers, the nation was at a crossroads. How would so many detached houses be built? In hindsight, it is clear that the decisions made to resolve the postwar housing crisis have had a lasting effect on American landscape, culture, economics, and politics. Practices introduced to resolve an immediate shortage were so effective that they evolved into the conventions and norms of production for the forty-five million new single-family detached houses built over the next half-century.

After 1945, careful debate and exploration were abandoned in the rush to supply the postwar housing demand. Instead, an underlying belief in technological solutions led to the adoption of manufacturing models to increase the housing supply. Builders and developers focused on house designs whose forms were based upon cost-efficient production that favored limiting articulation—eliminating dormers, valleys, verandas, and internal corners—as well as reducing house size to the smallest volume possible. These houses were cast onto the land and erected by crews of specialized builders. Road networks were laid out to equitably subdivide a large parcel of land into similarly sized and proportioned lots. Each crew executed a particular task, moving from house site to house site and installing prefabricated components purchased in mass quantities. Houses were placed near the center of their lots like machines, spaced apart from each other to avoid interfering with each other's activities.

LEVITTOWN   Levittown, New York, exemplified building of this time. This Long Island community was planned and developed by Levitt and Sons on the basis of industrialized production techniques and minimal housing standards. Potato fields in southern Long Island were replaced with networks of streets that provided access to subdivided lots onto which model homes were placed. The vision for living in this community focused on the individual household—a nuclear family—and its house. The Levitt house sought to economize by mass-producing what was considered the minimum set of activity spaces required for a family. Based upon FHA standards, the original Levitt house was 750 square feet (25 feet × 30 feet) and contained a living room, an eat-in kitchen, two bedrooms, and a bath. This stripped-down dwelling was offered as a prototype, with four choices of exterior appearance (see figures 19–21).

19. House plan and section of an original Levittown model home.

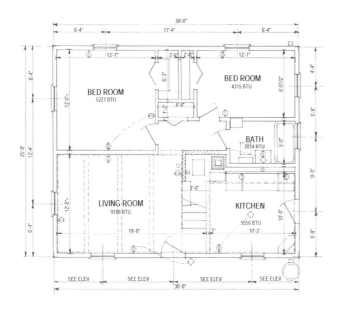

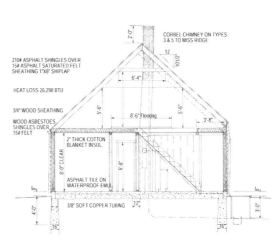

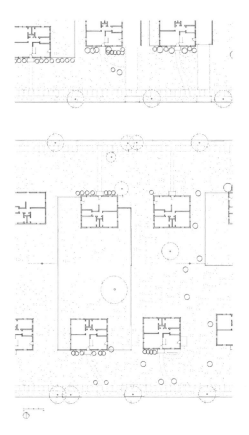

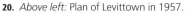

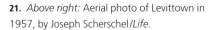

20. *Above left:* Plan of Levittown in 1957.

21. *Above right:* Aerial photo of Levittown in 1957, by Joseph Scherschel/*Life*.

There is little literature regarding the collective objectives or criteria for the planning of the first two thousand houses—the layout of the houses in relation to the site, to each other, or to the street. Given the sheer number of residents living in close proximity to one another (what Herbert Gans would later call a propinquity of neighboring[11]), it could be assumed that some sense of neighborhood and community would by necessity emerge. Nonetheless, the plans reveal that the connection of one household to others, to the landscape, or even to the back yard was neither considered nor valued. The house designs adequately fulfilled the FHA requirements, but once the houses were built in place, it became clear that use and view of the back yard were not design priorities. Bedrooms and the bathroom stretched across the back of the house, and only a few small bedroom windows looked out onto the back yard. The interior functioning of the house was emphasized rather than the relationships of a household to its social and physical landscape.[12] As summed up by one Levittown resident in 1950, "It's not a community that thinks much about what's going on outside."[13]

Without the foresight of testing or debate, developers erected vast numbers of houses. In Levittown alone, 17,447 houses were built in 7 square miles between 1947 and 1951.[14] To alleviate the postwar housing demand, developers advanced a volumetric approach to housing that minimized shared infrastructure. Unlike Radburn, Levittown had its public and collective components minimized to streets and lot subdivisions. The image of detached housing became rows of evenly spaced, nearly identical houses, centered in lots and strung out along streets. Financed by the government and invested in by families, this house-by-house approach came to dominate contemporary suburban development, with the alternatives for detached housing either forgotten or abandoned.

suburban settlement today

Suburban housing has evolved in several ways since the building of Levittown. In response to criticisms of the visual homogeneity of communities produced by identical houses and to expressed fears of the social uniformity that such communities might create, housing development again borrowed from manufacturing processes to personalize and increase variety in housing. Rather than being limited to a single prototypical house, as in Levittown, today's home owners choose from a selection of prototypes in the forms of "model homes." They can select a plot of land and a house model customized through options, finishes, equipment, and upgrades chosen prior to or during the construction process.

A second change is a noticeable increase in the size of houses and the return of articulated house forms. A contemporary "small" house has a substantially larger program than the postwar house: a living room, a dining room, an eat-in kitchen, a guest toilet, a family room, two to three bedrooms, two to three private bathrooms, a master bedroom with master bath, and a two- or three-car garage. Unlike the Levittown house, which had 750 square feet of living space, the "economy" house of today's suburbs often has 2,000 square feet of living space. Accompanying the larger house is an increase in the formal articulation of the house to bring both scale and variety to the house façade. With the price of land increasing, lot sizes decrease to contain costs. The net effect is larger houses on smaller lots.

At the same time, calls for "community" in suburban developments have returned. Thus, planning strategies aimed at engendering community, such as the designs for Columbia, Reston, Seaside, Kentlands, and Centennial, have been greeted with hope by the public, planners, administrators, and developers. In these places, the shared components of the Radburn plan have been replaced by bicycle paths or transformed into golf courses and commercial centers.

All of these trends accept a volumetric organization of suburban housing. The pattern of settlement continues to be a house-as-object approach, with homes placed on subdivided tracts facing an array of street patterns. The waste, isolation, and commodification that so many contemporary critics have identified as problems of American suburbs can all be traced to this form of settlement. As the following chapter will show, our reliance on prototypes underlies the way we see housing and propagates volumetric settings.

The great advantage in these machine made places lies with those who are just passing through, who don't have time to establish a more complex set of connections to a building or space. This may be helpful to a population on the move. But for those who spend time in these places, there is a quick decline of possibilities.

RALPH KNOWLES
"For Those Who Spend Time in a Place,"
Places 8 (Fall 1992)

chapter two | persistence of the box

THE POSTWAR SUBURBS HAVE BEEN CONTINUALLY SCRUTINIZED: WHO LIVES IN THE SUBURBS, HOW DO THEY LIVE, and is this way of living sustainable? The mass-produced housing environments of the 1950s suffered almost immediate condemnation for their visual monotony, social conformity, and isolated privacy. While detailed sociological study dispelled part of the critique as myth, other criticism faded as the housing delivery system evolved and the mass-produced suburban setting came to be commonly accepted. Still, the echoes of this critique reverberate, and today we question the loss of community, the inability of the suburbs to house diverse ways of living, and the waste of land and resources resulting from sprawl.

Despite the criticism, the demand for single-family detached housing is evident throughout the developed world. For most, the promises outweigh the criticism. The single-family house offers light and air from all sides. Access to the ground and to the street is direct, providing intimate connections with a range of "natural" settings—from tamed lawn and landscaped garden to rural trees and wild shrubs. Detachment provides households with the autonomy to build, maintain, remodel, buy, or sell their houses independent of one another.

With more than half the American population now living the suburban dream, calls for rejecting single-family detached lifestyles confront a culture centuries in the making. On the one hand, the postwar suburbs are cited as the cause of waste, isolation, and commodification in ways of living; on the other, their mass production has only made that culture more accessible. We cannot dismiss suburban living—that would be too easy and perhaps even disingenuous. Rather, what is needed is a critical framework that accepts detached housing as one mode of dwelling and shifts our focus from the object and its implied discontinuity to the fabric and its inherent continuity.

the model home

The notion of a plot of one's own runs deep, and we can arguably trace it back to the westward expansion of the United States. The National Survey's mapping of the public lands of the western states as a subdividable grid provided an equitable and democratic way to allocate land. With the passage of the Homestead Act in 1862, anyone could own a piece of land by living on and improving a plot for five years. As a result, vast portions of the American landscape became privatized for decentralized, individual use.

Civic leaders, in particular Thomas Jefferson, were concerned with the ways that American homesteaders lived and built their dwellings. The ramshackle homes built to stake claim to the land were not models for a stable citizenry. To influence but not regulate the domestic setting, civic leaders encouraged the use of pattern books of homes. These homes established the setting for the idealized life of the independent farmer and his family.[1] Thus, in the early days of American settlement, the seeds of contemporary suburban development were planted: a subdivision of land into relatively equal and therefore uniform lots, the private ownership and control of a plot of land, a lot-by-lot placement of houses, and the design of houses as model homes.

From a pattern that suggested an ideal from which each household could learn and adapt, the model home in the 1950s and 1960s became a prototype that was mass-produced and arrayed in neatly subdivided rows. Critics believed that the uniformity of the mass-produced setting led to a social homogeneity and conformity—that living in identical houses led to identical lives.[2] Lewis Mumford painted a vivid image of this setting as

> a multitude of uniform, unidentifiable houses, lined up inflexibly, in uniform distances, on uniform roads, in a treeless communal waste inhabited by people of the same class, the same income, the same age group, witnessing the same television performances, eating the same tasteless prefabricated food from the same freezers, conforming in every outward and inward respect to a common mold manufactured in the central metropolis.[3]

Suburbanites were ridiculed in literature, theater, and music for living in "little boxes made of ticky-tacky."[4]

The work of several sociologists[5] dispelled two of these myths. Their studies revealed that there was much more distinctiveness and difference among suburbanites' ways of living than was portrayed in the literature of the 1950s and 1960s, thereby proving that moving to the suburbs did not increase tendencies toward conformity. As a result, formal determinism was also dispelled—the form of a house did not prescribe its use. Even though the dread of conformity as a result of suburban living proved to be unfounded, the visual monotony of these prototype suburbs was undeniable. After the initial postwar rush, housing developers recognized the need for more choice, both to increase the visual variety between homes and to respond to the consumer.

To achieve variety, the techniques of mass production and mass marketing were again applied to the house. Today, housing production is based on sets of model homes, introducing more choices for home buyers yet still affording economies of scale to the developer. Variety within a neighborhood is introduced through the selection of models by prospective home owners, resulting in a random distribution of houses. Or, speculatively, different model homes are distributed on adjacent lots by the developer. Each model home is further personalized through subsets of options, typically for interior furnishings and equipment. In some communities, exterior options are also available, further increasing visual variety within a neighborhood of houses.

The model home, by definition, is a home that is intended to be used on many sites. From a design perspective, it is a prototype. To compensate for the unknown setting, a variety of approaches can be taken. First, a house can be designed solely for internal coherence—placing windows and doors that connect to the outside in a way that makes sense in terms of the internal logic of the house's program and rooms. Second, normative assumptions can be made about the future setting of a house—the most common scenario includes a street and front yard to one side, a rear yard that adjoins a neighbor's rear yard on the opposite side, and two houses flanking the two remaining sides. Prototypes designed to meet these conditions tend to have more openings to the front and rear yards and solid or nearly solid walls facing both side yards. A third approach is to compensate for the unknown future setting by inwardly orienting all activities. At its extreme, this results in courtyard houses in which all openings face a central, outdoor space and solid walls surround the exterior perimeter of the house. Most prototypical designs use some combination of all three approaches. In all cases, design actions stop at the outer boundary of the house, reinforcing the shell of the house as separation between house and setting.

Today, model homes are invariably located somewhat in the middle of their lots, following a pattern of centering based on a real estate rationale. A house is the most expensive item that most people purchase, so it is not surprising that home owners want to protect the value of their houses. Since the current structure of the suburbs is defined only by streets and lot subdivisions, value is most affected by changes on adjacent lots. Without a known structure for change and growth, each home owner minimizes the potential effects that can come from any direction by maximizing the distance and therefore the autonomy from adjoining lots.

Homes focused on their interiors and placed in the centers of equally sized plots produce an all-too-familiar image: they sit as objects, each discrete and discontinuous from the others and from its setting. We inherited this house-by-house production of the residential setting from the postwar rush to build, and its volumetric structuring has been the source of reverberating criticisms.

ossified dwelling

Whether suburban housing is accused of conformity, monotony, uniformity, or homogeneity, an underlying critique is that it places severe limits on the way we live. The source of this limitation is not the detached house but the volumetric production of houses as prototypes or "models."

Developers create basic house models by identifying markets, defining the lifestyles of those markets, and programming spaces for the targeted lifestyles. Normative assumptions about ways of living direct the design of spaces—their sizes, configurations, and adjacencies. For example, a common assumption about a nuclear family is that it needs children's sleeping areas. This activity, sleeping, is contained in spaces called bedrooms, each containing a bed, a closet, a dresser, and perhaps a work or play area. These assumed furnishings are arranged until an optimal configuration can be reached, the optimum defined by functional arrangement and minimal square footage within a generally rectangular space. The simple orthogonal configuration aids in aggregating various rooms within the house. In contemporary programming, sleeping is a "private" activity and is thus grouped away from the "public" activities of entertaining and dining. Bedroom windows are generally small, with waist-high sills that protect occupants' privacy while providing light and view. Each assumption tends to increase the specificity of a space for a prescribed activity.

This is not to say that other activities cannot take place within the room, but its potential for other uses diminishes. When every room is designed for an assumed activity, arguments about conformity and homogeneity ring true. Not only do new suburban communities target and attract similar lifestyles, but the existing housing stock is less able to absorb new or changing household structures because of a programmatically driven, functional approach to house design.

If changes cannot be absorbed within the house, some residents choose to enlarge a house to accommodate new needs. Yet the exterior spaces of volumetric suburbs also resist change. Some limit growth through a simple

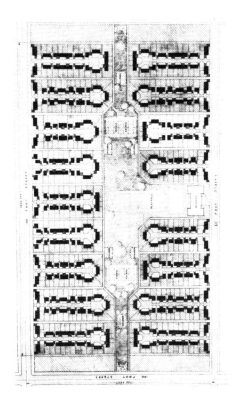

22. In this early study for Radburn, the designers used the volume of the houses to assemble the site plan. "Theoretical Study of a Superblock Dated January 17, 1928," by Clarence S. Stein.

lack of dimension in the lot. When houses are tightly packed and the yards are minimized, no additions can be made. Other yards are seen solely as moats of protection, rings of land that are neutral to growth and provide no suggestions to direct the further use of the land. With each house inwardly organized, the structure of the house and lot eliminates physical clues, strategies, and directions for outward expansion.

To return to the example of Radburn: its volumetric design approach is integral to both its planning success and its weakness. Residents routinely complain about the small size of the houses.[6] As described in the previous chapter, the form of community is built from the arrangement of houses as volumes (figure 22). At an average of 1,400 square feet, the original houses are all small by today's standards. The typical house has a living area, a kitchen, and an eating area on the ground floor and two bedrooms and a bath on the second. Although many of the houses sit on lots large enough to hold additions, covenants limit the scope and type of permissible construction. The only sanctioned exterior changes are additions above the garages, the enclosing of side porches, and the enclosing or rebuilding of the open porches that face the walkway. In essence, the covenants maintain the original volumes of the houses. For Radburn to retain its form of community, particularly the cul-de-sacs, the houses' volumes cannot change.

The shells of suburban houses have also become more physically intransigent to change. Structural bearing, thermal mediation, heating and air conditioning, plumbing, electricity, view, and air are all controlled within the depth of a stud wall. The collapse of so many systems into one thin layer makes it difficult to reconfigure a house without interrupting and rerouting many systems.

With housing that resists both change and growth, the most common way to accommodate evolving lifestyles is to "trade up"—from starter home to family home to home-office to retirement home. A culture of moving and trading reinforces the view of house as commodity, a material good to be bought and sold. Residents often find themselves in a bind, choosing between space or place—moving away for more appropriate space or choosing to stay in a place in spite of the inconveniences.

isolated dwelling

In 1961, Jane Jacobs characterized suburban living as isolated and privatized.[7] Jacobs's concern was how residents lived—how connections to a place were diminished by the lack of public interaction, diversity of activities, and density of population in the suburbs. Her criticisms, directed primarily against planning that increased the specialization of land uses,

23. Isolation of dwelling from the street.

still resonate in contemporary assessments of suburbia as characterized by a "weakened sense of community, . . . a tendency for social life to become 'privatized' and . . . a reduced feeling of concern and responsibility among families for their neighbors."[8] Concern about suburban residents' isolation and limited public life persists.[9] Again, the criticism should be directed not at detached housing but at its volumetric structuring, which minimizes ways of sharing.

A volumetric approach to housing emphasizes the house's perimeter as a separation between public and private as well as interior and exterior space. By defining autonomy and privacy with bounding forms, volumetric suburbs isolate households within shells. Ways of living are now centripetal, centered inside the house at the hearth or television or in the private back yard. As the variety of model homes in a setting increases, with each house containing distinct and discrete ways of dwelling, the discontinuities in the setting intensify. Gone are the broader views of the landscape, shared spaces such as sidewalks, and common thresholds such as porches. Shared understandings about living in a place are disappearing (figure 23). As Kenneth Jackson wrote, "There are few places as desolate and lonely as a suburban street on a hot afternoon."[10]

wasted land

Recent criticism is directed toward the environmental consequences of suburban sprawl.[11] Land and energy are no longer seen as limitless resources. As the suburban housing base expands, more agricultural lands are lost, as are the diversity and depth of ecosystems. Reliance upon the automobile adds to resource depletion and pollution. Concerns about both the short- and long-term consequences of these patterns of sprawl have led to planning alternatives that limit the extent of suburban growth and require an increase in suburban density. Unfortunately, the extensive

chapter two

24a, b, c, d, e. Residual spaces in volumetric settings.

application of volumetric approaches for denser residential settings only intensifies the wasted, residual quality of suburban outdoor spaces (as seen in figures 24a–e).

When model homes that have been designed without consideration of their particular setting are finally built, the consequences become immediately apparent. These programmatic prototypes miss the advantages of a site's particular conditions, from common situations such as corner lots or rear alleys to specific views, microclimates, and unique topographies. Houses whose forms are based primarily on internal coherence end up either with two blank walls facing each other or with windows looking into their neighbors' bedroom, living room, or garbage. A person entertaining in his living area looks into a neighbor's bedroom; an animated household at dinner looks across to a neighbor struggling with her taxes at the dining room table. Common remedies to these conflicts, such as curtains and shrubs, close off light and view, further accentuating the house's shell.

To intensify the use of suburban land, lot sizes are shrinking. The land around a house is often a minimally sized skirt—20 feet in front, 25 feet in back, and 3 to 5 feet on either side. As the spaces between houses get smaller, the leftover character of the interstices is exacerbated. At best, these residual spaces become landscaped buffers between neighbors; at worst, they are trashed and unkempt storage spaces. In either case, the spaces between houses are neither part of a house nor part of the larger landscape. This inattentive use of land generated by volumetric development contributes to the condemnation of suburban sprawl.

persistence of the volumetric

As our national love-hate relationship with suburbs continues, ever-larger regions are covered with disjointed and discontinuous housing. Commentaries about the suburbs categorically accept a volumetric—house-by-house and tract-by-tract—production of our suburbs, even among architects and planners. This acceptance has eliminated careful formal analysis and architectural alternatives. If architects are to reinsert themselves into the debate over the physical form of suburban housing, they must first recognize the design profession's contribution to the persistence of volumetric settings by examining the methods that constitute the practice of suburban design.

To resolve the complexities of dwelling, professionals seek approaches and tools that clarify the issues. A volumetric conception of the suburbs corresponds with a simple, hierarchic segmentation of professional practice. Responsibility for the form of our residential settings is divided among specialists—the interior designer, the architect, the landscape architect, the transportation planner, the urban planner—each of whom designs his or her own area: the house interior, the house, the yard, the street, the city. As each profession focuses on its own solutions, the limits of responsibility separate house from yard, yard from street, and neighbor from neighbor. In trying to simplify the problem, professionals make the design of the dwelling experience discontinuous at each environmental level.

Zoning regulations also institutionalize volumetric views of the suburbs. These local controls explicitly protect the public welfare and implicitly protect land and house values. They have the unintended consequence of sustaining a view of houses as discrete objects by governing houses' positions through setback requirements that define the minimum distances between a house and its property lines. Typically, more dimension is allotted to front and back yards; side yards are smaller but are equal to each other. These setbacks position houses in the center of their plots, independent and isolated.

Likewise, home owners' agreements and covenants control commonly held areas that are not under public jurisdiction. This common domain frequently extends to the exterior façades of the houses, since they serve as the walls of the public and community-owned spaces. Again, these covenants implicitly accept and sustain a volumetric structure of a setting by assuming that dwelling occurs within a fixed shell. Regulations can be applied to the outside of a shell, but interior space is under the home owner's control. Designs that build a collective image of a neighborhood through the exteriors of houses must control and conserve a volumetric structure.

An argument against the volumetric suburb is not an argument against enclosed spaces. Indeed, a sense of enclosure is both a pleasurable and a necessary thing. But the categorical acceptance of volumetric structuring as the basis of detached-housing form and settlement has led to fragmented, unintelligible, and largely underused landscapes that constitute a significant proportion of today's residential environment. Designers extend that practice with the uncritical use of volumetric concepts such as hierarchy and massing. Instead, an approach is needed that sees the continuous nature of everyday activities and structures dwelling in a contextual way—as a fabric.

It took me years before it occurred to me, but I finally started thinking about houses as boxes: four sides, one lid, one bottom joined together. I don't know why it took me so long before I thought of this. It seems so much easier to understand houses now that I have. I hold in my mind the simple picture of a cardboard box. A box, let's say, that I would use to ship something to a friend. I pick a fairly heavy cardboard box, one with sides that will not easily cave in, I reinforce the seams with strapping tape. . . .

See why thinking of a house as a box is helpful? It puts things in perspective. What you want is a good box, one that will last and is comfortable to spend time in. It sits solidly on its spot. It won't sink or float off when it's wet. Its sides and corners won't bend or buckle. Inside it is warm, good light comes in and there are no leaks.

Houses are boxes that we go into and live. We close the door to our box and we are warm and dry and we can sleep. And wild animals can't get in.

ANET TARPOFF AND PAT TALBERT

"A House Is Just a Box," real estate section of the *Hills Publication,* January 11, 1996

chapter three | defining dwelling

HOW WE DEFINE *DWELLING* IS KEY TO RECONSIDERING SUBURBAN SPACE AS A FABRIC. In design, our deliberations over dwelling must encompass more than just programs and lifestyles, both of which are too static to explain dwelling. Dwelling defined as an ideal or as a set of normative patterns for living oversimplifies and limits the possibilities for ways of living. Instead, dwelling should be considered as involving creative and complex acts. More than a sheltering of activities, it is a multifaceted phenomenon that brings together where we live and how we live, each informing and changing the other. The creativity in dwelling is found in the ever-changing discourses that residents conduct between their physical place and their ways of living; its complexity is derived from the diversity of those discourses. Thus, the term *dwelling* is simultaneously noun and verb, the interaction between our places and our ways of dwelling.

The dwelling discourse allows individuals to see the form of a place through their activities. Herman Hertzberger describes this process as one of "reading," in which residents bring their desires and habits to inform their perception of the built environment: "Form can be vested with meaning, but can also be divested of it, by the use to which the form is put and by the values that are attributed and added to it, or indeed removed from it—all depending on the way in which users and form interact."[1]

Form in this dialogue is not deterministic—spatial configuration is not coupled with a specific behavior, just as a change in function does not always require an alteration of form. But, at the same time, *where* we live is not independent of *how* we live—the form of a place is not irrelevant to its inhabitation. For instance, the activity of dining evokes a range of possible places for eating, just as a bay window suggests a variety of ways for occupying that space (figures 25a–b and 26a–b). For designers, what is significant is competence in designing for a range of readings—an ability to embed a creative rather than a prescriptive discourse between form and use.

25a, b. Occupying a bay window.

26a, b. Dining.

The discourse of dwelling is learned. We learn about dwelling from our past experiences as a part of some households and as an observer of others; we shift and redirect our customs on the basis of new awareness, needs, and desires.[2] These experiences and desires not only guide how we choose to live but also predispose our responses to particular spaces, forms, and organizations.[3] That is to say, the ways that we read spaces are learned, and this learning leads us, consciously or unconsciously, to seek, construct, or read in places a correspondence to the way we live.

Dwelling is temporal. Our reading of the environment continually changes to suit our emerging requirements, reflecting the ongoing effect of learning. The ways in which we live change in cycles—daily, seasonal, life stage, and generational. As a result, our relationship to dwelling is not fixed or static. At the time when a reading no longer fits a place, changes are made—from rearranging to remodeling, adding, or moving.

The complexity of dwelling is pronounced in the United States due to the diversity of cultural patterns based on rituals, traditions, socioeconomic groups, age, religion, and desires. Each person's way of living is a unique combination of shared patterns, resulting in a vast multitude of ways of living. There is common agreement that much of our suburban housing stock constrains the diversity of lifestyles, and this sense of incongruity is augmented by the acknowledgment that there is no longer an ideal or set of ideals about how we are to live.[4] Rather than depending on our ability to adapt, can we design suburban housing that offers more ways to accommodate complex and changing definitions of dwelling? To answer this, designers need to turn away from market approaches and instead nurture their belief and competence in the life of forms.

defining dwelling

dwelling as use

Every setting has structure, a form, that is inhabited, interpreted, and read. Our use of settings is always changing, and the form is continually being reread and reinterpreted. Yet, at any moment in time, a setting needs to be complete in its inhabitation. To accommodate this dialogue, our settings need to support multiple associations and uses. To accommodate the temporality of dwelling, a structure must easily give up a particular reading and take on a new one. The form of our settings should not be neutral, easily accommodating new functions but giving no suggestion or association, nor should our settings be so functionally specified that they cannot accommodate new meanings. Our settings need to suggest and

27a, b. *Top:* Pueblo Ribera—hearths as read by two different households.

28a, b. *Bottom:* Sachs Apartments—edge of room used for dining or work.

29a, b. *Top:* Sachs Apartments—edge of room used for sleeping or work.

30a, b. *Middle:* Sachs Apartments—zone along the fireplace used for work or living.

31a, b. *Bottom:* Pueblo Ribera—original sleeping loft converted to bedroom.

remind us of ways we have lived, or would like to live, and should allow us to revisit our associations without having to completely change the form of the house (figures 27–31). An alcove of a room holds a desk, then a sofa, then a table. The fireplace hearth not only delimits an area around the fire but also can be a seat, a display area, a structural support, a definition of spatial direction, and a shared element among neighbors. The yard can be used for a car, a picnic table, a household garden, and a community park. In this way, the forms of our residential settings support dwelling.

dwelling as collective

Two pairs of terms are often used interchangeably: *public* and *private* are equated with *collective* and *individual*. When designers equate them, individual activities are private spaces and collective activities are public spaces. This is a polarized, black-or-white interpretation of how we share our residential settings, and a volumetric approach to design maintains and intensifies the separation.

As a way of living, *individual* refers to the condition of recognizing one's distinctness within a larger whole. Dwelling is individual. The space of individual activity is a recognizable territory or domain intended for the use of a person or a distinct group of residents, such as a household, within the larger setting. An individual space is part of the collective setting. Because, in this spatial construct, an individual or individuals are located within a collective, the definitions of *individual* and *collective* differ from those of *private* and *public*. *Private* and *public* are relative terms that describe a condition of exclusion or inclusion of others. A private space is a territory of controlled accessibility and limited visibility to others, as opposed to a public space that readily admits. In a house, the living area may be public compared to a bedroom, but the same living area is private in relation to the street.

Distinguishing between these paired characteristics is important. An individual space is not necessarily a private space; likewise, a collective space is not necessarily a public space. For example, a bench in an open park is an individual space; a single person occupies it but does so in the presence of, and as part of, the public domain. In a living area of a house, a bay window seat can be read as an individual space, but it is still part of the larger space of its room. It is a private space as seen from the street; it is part of the public space as seen from within the house.

When privacy and individuality are equated rather than seen as overlapping, all individual spaces are designed as private spaces. A place for an individual to sleep is turned into a private room. The domain for an individual household is translated to a private domain, with privacy defended at the perimeter of the house or lot. Likewise, when the collective environment is equated with the public environment, only centralized and infrastructural elements are considered for the building of a shared environment. When individual dwelling is privatized and collective dwelling is made public, relations in the suburbs are less complex, more uniform and discrete. Lost are possibilities to construct collective environments through a weaving of individual activities and the potential to share without forsaking privacy and autonomy.

dwelling as a fabric

Another confusion in defining *dwelling* stems from assuming that *inside* means *interior*, that dwelling is a building. Although there are climatic reasons for distinguishing between interior and exterior, good dwelling spaces are all sensed as being inside[5]—inside a room, inside a house, inside a yard, inside a street, inside a neighborhood, and inside a landscape (figures 32a–e). As such, the experience of dwelling is continuous; it has the potential to occur throughout any setting. Dwelling should be considered a physical and spatial continuum that we live in and move through. This continuum, often referred to as a fabric,[6] is a continuous structure of spaces and forms that we experience, read, and inhabit.

32a, b, c, d, e. In the fabric of the setting. *From top left,* room, house, yard, street, and city (Sachs Apartments).

In contemporary suburban design, not all parts of dwelling are equally valued. With most design consideration given to house and street, the dwelling potential of much of our suburban settings is diminished—the spaces between houses, yards, and neighborhoods are often overlooked. In a fabric, structuring the continuities is as important as defining the discontinuities, and the individual and collective discourses are seen as forming and informing each other.

We are dealing with activities related to building and dwelling. It [dwelling] is about personal considerations and decisions, the formulating of one's own desires, and the coming to a judgment about a given work. It concerns the assessing and choosing of innumerable small details, the manifestation of preferences and whims. It concerns the freedom to know better than others, or to do the same as others. It has to do with the care to maintain, or the carelessness about private possessions, with the sudden urge to change as well as the stubborn desire to conserve and keep. It is related to the need to display and to create one's own environment, but also the desire to share that of others, or to follow in a fashion. The need to give one's personal stamp is as important as the inclination to be unobtrusive. In short, it all has to do with the need for a personal environment where one can do as one chooses.

N. JOHN HABRAKEN
Supports: An Alternative to Mass Housing
(London: Architectural Press, 1972 [1961 in Dutch])

chapter four | seeing suburban dwelling as a fabric

A VIEW OF DWELLING AS A FABRIC—AS CONTINUOUSLY AND POSITIVELY OCCUPYING THE BUILT ENVIRONMENT— has a long tradition in the study of cities. The suburbs, though, have largely been omitted from this history. Perhaps this is because the building of a residential settlement by aggregating individual houses appears to be such a simple task. Yet design for good suburban dwelling is no less complex in its demands for weaving the collective with the individual than design for urban dwelling and perhaps is even more complex when the outdoor landscape is integrated. Because the problem appears to be so simple, the tools by which suburbs have been depicted have been correspondingly simplistic. Looking at the continuities of fabrics in the design of detached houses makes it possible to see the suburbs in a new light.

Implicit in this discussion is the importance of representation in design. Representation structures our awareness. The designer uses representation as a surrogate for the real environment and in doing so reveals aspects of a problem.[1] Thus, representation enables design by emphasizing a particular view; it can also constrain design through what is not revealed. In a reconsideration of the suburbs as fabrics, approaches to representing detached dwelling must be evaluated as to their aptitude to reveal qualities of a house as part of a setting.

Seeing detached dwelling as a fabric requires means of representation that capture the continuities and shared characteristics of the built environment. There are three broad approaches for depicting these settlement patterns: built-unbuilt, hierarchic, and experiential.[2] Architects' and planners' reliance upon the first two modes aggravates suburban problems of waste, commodification, and isolation. To weave dwelling into a suburban landscape, designers need to be able to see and argue for the experience of living in a place.

built-unbuilt representation

A common representation of the built environment is that of built-unbuilt space, also referred to as figure-ground (figure 33). Typically, built space is rendered as the figure, with unbuilt space left as the background, which is then read as "ground." From this representation, patterns and shapes emerge that are useful for both description and design. In the textures, the overall structure of a place can be read as well as its particular details—boundaries, districts, and both the continuity and singularity of buildings and open spaces. This kind of representation characterizes the reciprocity between built and unbuilt spaces as shaped.

A richer understanding of the patterns can be conveyed through additional overlays of information—public buildings, dates of construction, ownership, building heights, or use—on the built-unbuilt plan. For example, Camillo Sitte transformed the plan as a representation by toning the built spaces gray, the churches black, and the unbuilt public spaces white (figure 34).[3] Through this additional emphasis, Sitte observed and outlined principles for city planning in which he argued for continuity, or shared characteristics of settings, through the shaping of city plazas and streets.

In the design of residential environments, N. John Habraken used a built-unbuilt plan on which outdoor, thematic spaces that shared patterns or characteristics were toned light gray; built, thematic spaces black; and

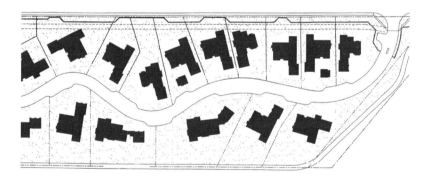

33. Built-unbuilt plan of a California suburb.

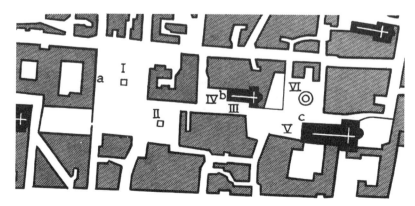

34. Built-unbuilt plan of a piazza in Lucca, by Camillo Sitte.

chapter four

35. Plan of Schilders area, The Hague, by H. Reyenga (Habraken 1973).

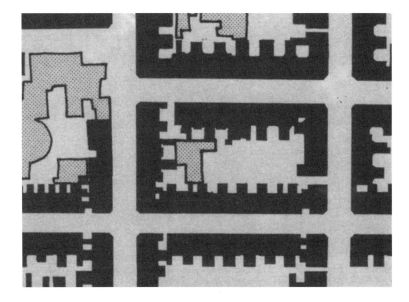

36. "Houston, Texas—August, 1885—Section 12," by the Sanborn Map Company.

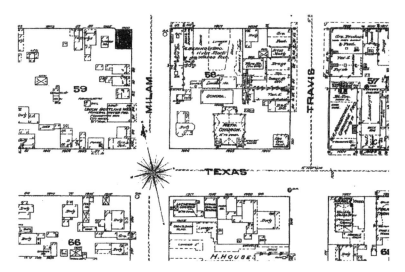

nonthematic elements (built or unbuilt) dark gray (figure 35).[4] Through this rendering, Habraken distinguished between elements that were continuous in the sense of having a similar nature and placement and elements that were unique and discrete from their surroundings.

The plans of the Sanborn Map Company recorded the "distribution and characteristics of urban buildings" for fire insurance companies.[5] On a built-unbuilt plan (figure 36), color tones indicated materials of construction, and sets of symbols and numbers described the three-dimensional characteristics of the buildings' mass. The unbuilt environment was described with property lines, dimensions, ownership labels, and some infrastructural information. Although these plans lack the immediate visual clarity of a two-tone built-unbuilt plan, the additional information and three-dimensional characteristics of a setting required by fire insurance companies have proved to be useful for designers as well.

Just these few examples illustrate the rich informational potential of built-unbuilt plans. Nonetheless, the designer also needs to ask what this filter conceals. Design with built-unbuilt plans draws attention to shaping reciprocities between indoor and outdoor space, but the clarity of the representation eliminates spatial information critical to the consideration of any reciprocity. The relationships of interior spaces—either within one building or from one building to another—as well as interior-to-exterior relationships are not described. A border between built and unbuilt space is shown as a thin line. In the process of designing, the border too often is translated into a wall or façade, separating indoor spaces from outdoor and eliminating transitions.

hierarchic representation

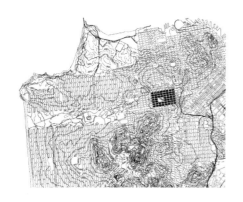

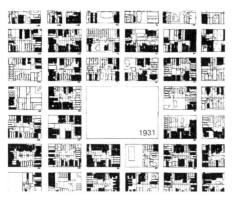

An essential experiential quality of any environment is that of being "inside"—inside a room, inside a building, inside the street, inside the block, inside the city, inside the region, and so on. In the study of fabrics, one way to describe this quality is to associate each scale of the environment with a different method of representation. The city scale is drawn in one way, commonly as a street plan; the district or block is rendered another way, often as a built-unbuilt plan; and buildings are described with plans showing interior partitions. This has the effect of nesting or telescoping, in which one zooms in and out for different scales of information.

Hierarchic approaches represent a fabric's continuous qualities by exemplifying, so that a plan at one scale serves as an example for a larger area. This is extremely useful in districts composed of repetitive street patterns and distinct building typologies. For example, in describing the fabric of San Francisco and its ability to support change, Anne Vernez Moudon represented historical changes in the city at three levels (figures 37a–c).[6] The city scale was described with streets and other transportation networks at various points in time, the district scale through built-unbuilt plans of the block habitation at three time periods, and the

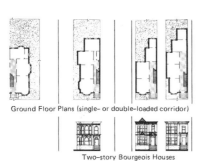

Ground Floor Plans (single- or double-loaded corridor)

Two-story Bourgeois Houses

37a, b, c. Three scales of San Francisco. *Top to bottom:* "The San Francisco Peninsula," "Alamo Square 1931," and "Typology of House Forms and Lots—Wide and Narrow Single Lots," by Anne Vernez Moudon.

chapter four

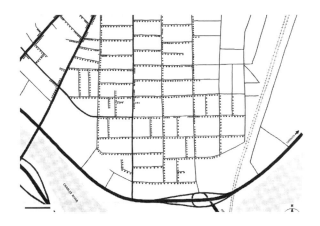

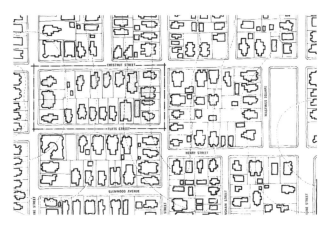

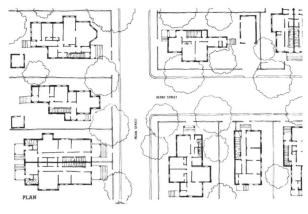

house scale through a description of the house types and their physical and positional variations. Implicit in Moudon's argument was that the urban fabric supported change and variation through the hierarchy of scales and the use of typology.

Another example of this hierarchic representation is found in Horacio Caminos's work in Cambridgeport.[7] Caminos used four scales to describe dwelling environments: the locality, a segment of the locality, a dwelling group, and a typical dwelling unit (figures 38a–d). Embedded within the dwelling unit was a room-level description that showed the furniture layout of one set of residents. Caminos then applied his method of representation to eight urban dwelling environments in the Boston area and in four Latin American cities.

As with built-unbuilt representation, projecting with hierarchic representations of the environment conceals some relations. In the process of designing, interventions tend to be made on a level-by-level basis to match each scale of the description. Spatial relations between levels must be held within the intelligence of the designer or ignored—even if momentarily—while designing. This gap between levels commonly results in design practices in which each scale is resolved independently of the others. For instance, an urban plan is developed without information about building plans, or a building is designed without regard to its larger context. Too often, the result is the dissolution of a setting: buildings stand discrete from each other and apart from their surroundings. Ironically, though the character of continuity in the fabrics of San Francisco and Cambridgeport is aptly described with hierarchic representations, the design of shared characteristics across a setting is not an inherent outcome.

38a, b, c, d. Hierarchic plans of Cambridgeport. *Top to bottom:* "Locality Circulation Plan," "Locality Segment Plan," "Dwelling Group," and "Typical Dwelling," by Horacio Caminos, John Turner, and John Steffian.

American suburbs, dominated by hierarchic approaches in design and development, provide a case study in this disintegration of a setting. Typically, design of a suburban neighborhood is represented through a "master plan" (figure 39) that positions the infrastructure, lays out transportation networks, and parcels land into smaller lots for individual ownership. Houses are distributed on a lot-by-lot basis. In a new development, a future home owner selects a lot as well as a house from a group of model homes available from the developer or from a vast array of model home catalogues (figure 40). In more speculative situations, a developer prearranges the model homes for a targeted market. This approach is hierarchic: the community is designed with street and plot plans; neighborhoods are defined

39. Master plan of a development in California.

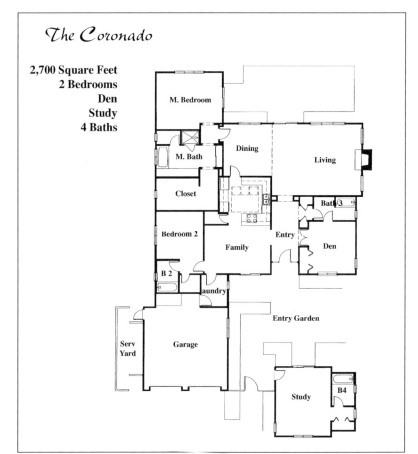

40. Plan of one model home in this development.

41. The design arguments embedded in the built-unbuilt plan are similarly explored with the massing model.

with built-unbuilt plans, including footprint, land use, or roof plans; and houses are designed with architectural plans.

In this hierarchy, information about a building and information about its context are separated into two views. As a result, house-to-house relations are not transparent, and house design can evolve independent of the context. This acontextual proposition matches model home design. As described in an earlier chapter, model homes have come to be defined either as houses without a particular context or as houses that can be built in any context. Spatial relations to the setting are intentionally eliminated or ignored. In the design of model homes, activities tend to be inwardly focused and self-referential to compensate for the unknown conditions of the future site. Privacy is controlled at the surface of the house, with the outer shell or volume of the house emphasized as a boundary between inside and outside. The boundaries and acontextual views of dwelling embedded in the hierarchic, master plan/model home approach lead to a volumetric structuring of the suburbs. For clarity of argument, only plan representations are described in this chapter, but it is important to note that this volumetric form also corresponds to another standard tool of housing design—the massing model (figure 41).

experiential representation

A third approach to representation describes the everyday experience of being within a setting. Experiential representation argues for rendering a fabric as one would dwell and move through it, with the experience defined again as a state of being inside—inside the room, the building, the street, the block. It differs from a hierarchic representation in that the continuity of the experience is rendered at one scale.

The name most notably associated with this kind of representation is that of Giambattista Nolli. In his 1748 plan of Rome (figure 42), he

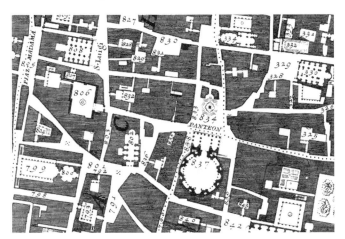

42. Rome in 1748, by Giambattista Nolli.

described the public experience of being in the city by leaving the publicly accessible interior spaces untoned, making them continuous with the unbuilt public space of the ground. This kind of representation describes the experience of the city as one of moving between plaza or street and the interior spaces of public buildings. The consistency of a built-unbuilt plan is forsaken, since in most places unbuilt space does not equate with public space, or built space with private.

This experiential representation is further articulated in Klaus Herdeg's work on formal structure,[8] in which plans present differing perspectives of the same setting. His plans of Maidan-I-Shah, Iran (figure 43), describe the overlapping domains of people of various social positions: visitors, citizens, civil servants, clergy, and royalty. The experience of the fabric differs depending upon individual perspective—as a member of the clergy, civil servant, or citizen.

When every portion of the setting is spatially described at one scale— indoor and outdoor as well as public and private—the experiential representation holds the most information. Referred to as "tissue" by Habraken,[9] *tessuto* by Cannigia,[10] and "dwelling group" by Caminos,[11] this kind of rendering describes both the general character and the particular conditions of the dwelling environment. From these plans, patterns can be read, and from these patterns emerge formal typologies, themes, and systems.

43. Maidan-I-Shah, by Klaus Herdeg: "Different Perceptions of the Maidan."

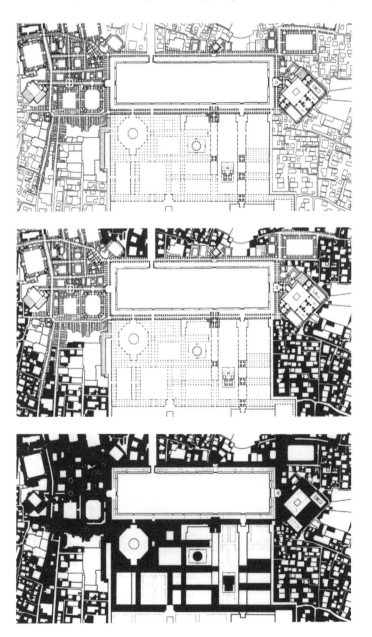

44. *Top left:* Venice, by Saverio Muratori: "Tav. VII—Quartiere di S. Cangiano—S. Maria Nova—Situazione Attuale."

45. *Top right:* Detail of "Area of Avenue Victor-Hugo. Engineering Structure," by Stanford Anderson.

For example, Saverio Muratori documented large portions of the Venetian fabric, reconstructing several stages of development in order to understand the city's structure and growth and to develop a theory to guide the city's transformation (figure 44).[12] Another example is Stanford Anderson's research on the ecological modeling of cities. In particular, his work in Paris (figure 45) depicted various systems in the dwelling environment, such as engineering structure and spaces of public, dwelling, and occupational claim.[13]

Still another layer of information needs to be added to architectural plans that describes a momentary reading of a setting as it holds everyday activities. For in the conduct of everyday life, people do more than move through space. To study dwelling requires knowledge of how the setting is used and inhabited. Cultural anthropologists[14] and vernacular historians[15] commonly relate use to the spatial form of a house by studying the artifacts of dwelling—how artifacts are positioned to use, to remind, to control, and to personalize. In this book, the study of spatial patterning is extended from the house to the setting by recording both interior and exterior occupation of space on experiential plans (figure 46). In this way, concern for dwelling as a dialogue between activity and place is embedded within the representation.

Through experiential representation, one may move through streets into yards and into houses as well as rooms. One looks out from a bay window of a room to the street, to the neighbors, to rooms in the back of the

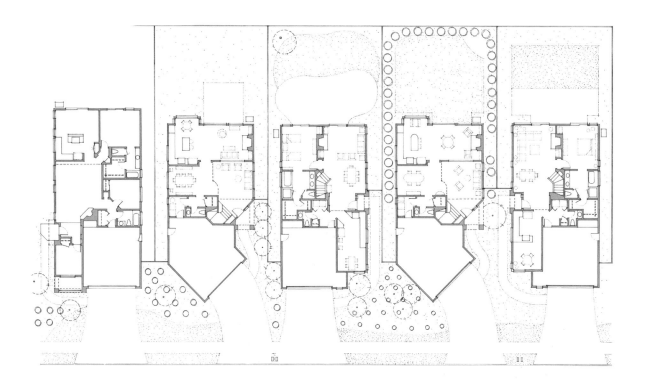

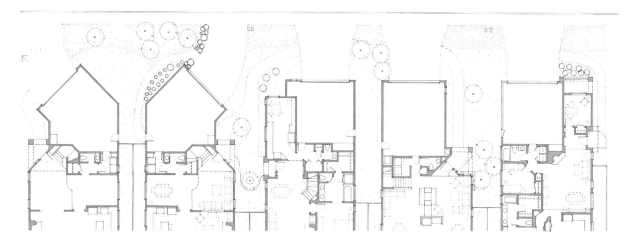

46. Clayton, California—as inhabited. This plan records *dwelling* as both a noun and a verb.

house and into the back yard. These relationships, not immediately transparent in built-unbuilt or hierarchic representations, are critical to suburban living.

Like other forms of representation, experiential representations need to be evaluated in terms of their constraints as projective tools. In design, experiential plans have two drawbacks: one, the density and completeness of the information; two, the limitations of a frame. The detailed level of information in experiential representation is both its strength and its weakness. When experiential representation is used to describe an existing

chapter four

place, the specificity of the information can mask a fabric's continuities and shared characteristics. When it is used in designing, the form of a place, as shown in the examples above, is at a stage of resolution that is too complete to be achieved in initial and intermediate stages of projection. Representations used early in the design process need to be generative, suggesting subsequent steps and raising additional areas of concern.

To both clarify and open this representation, attributes of housing design and planning can be represented as layers. Through this layering, each attribute can be highlighted for independent study as well as merged to show relationships with other layers. When layering is extended to the experiential plan, attributes are represented systemically across a setting—from house to house and from exterior to interior. In this way, the density of information in an experiential rendering can be clarified through layering, and these layers can be used for projection as well as analysis.[16] Five attributes are examined in this book: dimensions, access, claim, assemblage, and containment. Their definitions and layered representations are illustrated by two case studies—Levittown, Long Island, and the Sachs Apartments in Los Angeles (figures 47 and 48).

47. Levittown, Long Island.

48. The Sachs Apartments in Los Angeles.

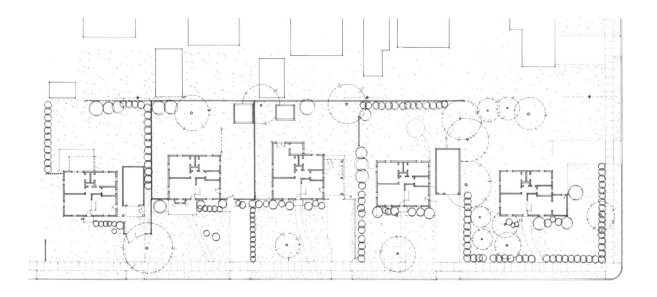

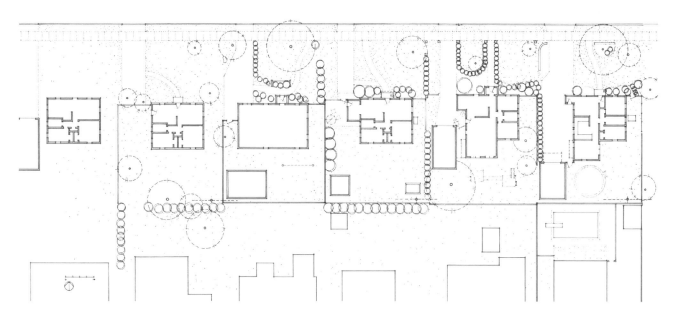

49. Levittown—inhabited.

mapping dwelling

Located on a steep hillside, the Sachs Apartments[17] are accessed by public footpaths that climb between the upper and lower streets. The apartments, stacked like steps, are organized in five buildings, and the units' entries are set at different levels along the footpaths. Although the complex falls outside the definition of single-family detached housing, the Sachs Apartments merit study because the density and organization of the complex fall at a cusp between detached and attached housing. Their

50. The Sachs Apartments—inhabited.

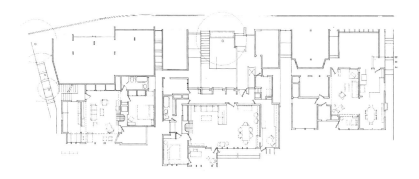

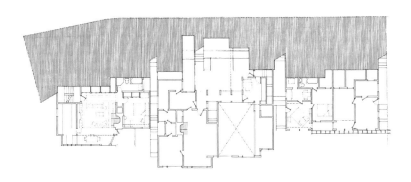

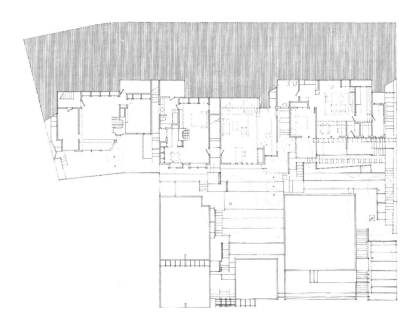

analysis provides key insights for seeing detached residential buildings as fabrics. Levittown[18] is described using the same systemic representation. A comparison of the mapping of their attributes (figures 49 and 50) provides a formal basis for a critical discussion of the suburbs.

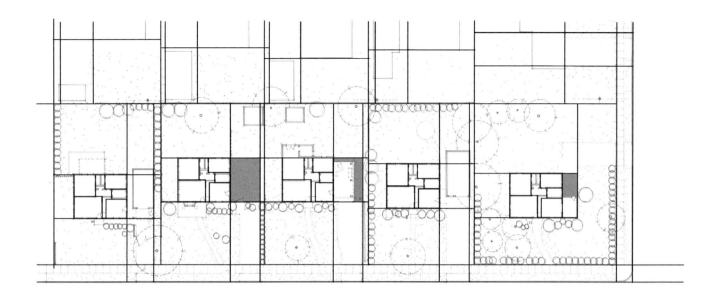

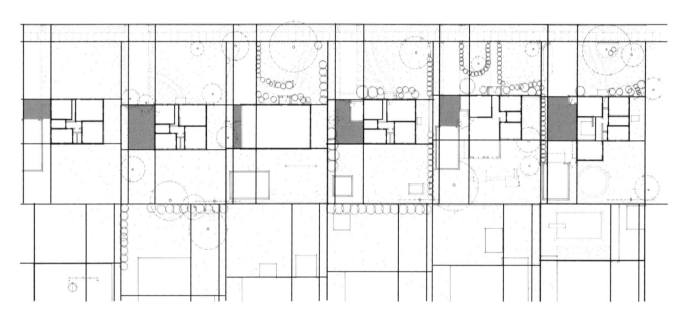

51. Levittown—dimensioned.

MAPPING DIMENSIONS *Dimensions* here refers to sizes of activity spaces and the organization of those sizes. Typically, dimensions in housing are functionally derived. Sizes are tied to configurations of furnishings for anticipated activities. These sizes are then organized by adjacencies of activities—what function should be adjacent to or removed from another.

In a systemic view of dimensions, the relations between sizes for activities are made more visible. That is, the dimensions of activities are seen and positioned in relation to other sizes in the setting, not just in relation to function. These dimensional overlays highlight two general kinds of activities: primary and personal.[19] Primary dimensions contain the uses

chapter four

52. The Sachs Apartments—dimensioned.

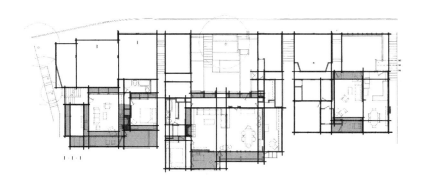

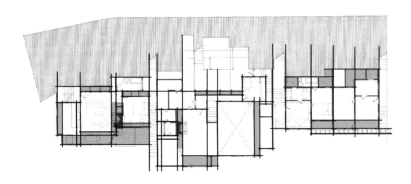

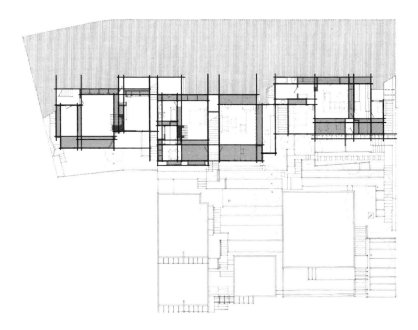

that require the largest areas and typically fulfill the requirements of a program. Activities that occupy these primary dimensions commonly include dining, preparing food, entertaining, sleeping, and bathing. Personal dimensions hold the smaller, but equally important, activities of a household. The activities in these dimensions tend to be individualized and unique to each household. Examples include talking on the phone, working at a desk, lounging with a book, storing or displaying personal goods, and so on. In determining room and house sizes, designers often combine primary with primary dimensions, combine primary with personal dimensions, or just use primary dimensions alone.

In dimensional overlays, untoned areas delineate the territories of primary activities; shaded areas highlight dimensions of personal uses. Reference lines emphasize where these territories meet and demarcate zones as well as shared alignments.

The two case studies (figures 51, page 56, and 52, page 57) illustrate the differences between dimensions that are either functionally or structurally derived. In Levittown, all interior dimensions are primary and organized on a room-by-room basis (figure 51). Between the house and its setting, there is only minimal dimensional structuring. The front façades of each house generally align to build the dimension of the front yards. As originally laid out, each house had one side yard of 10 feet and another side yard of 25 feet. The house was displaced toward one side to accommodate car parking on the lot. Over time, the dimension for the car has accommodated many of the additions to the Levitt house.

In the Sachs Apartments, primary and personal dimensions are interwoven throughout the breadth and depth of the setting (figure 52). The bands of personal spaces augment the primary sizes for a greater range of spatial readings. There are 2-foot zones both along the retaining wall against the hill and perpendicular to the hill, usually articulated with built-in furniture, shelves, closets, and overhead lighting. Along the edge that overlooks the hill, there is a 6- to 8-foot band, sized to hold personal activities such as eating, working, and lounging.

MAPPING ACCESS   *Access* is the space of moving—between, into, and through other spaces. It is a spatial connection between activities. Too often, access is seen solely as a route of travel between two activities, a path to get from here to there. This view is graphically depicted as a line of linkage that indicates the route. But access also can be seen as a journey, a way of moving within a setting—along a path and within activities—with opportunities for view, light, and an occasional conversation. A single line cannot describe the potential of access as a space or the contribution of its configuration and position to the overall experience. As an alternative, a systemic overlay highlights the space of access as well as the structural contribution of access to a setting. Thus, the toned areas in these overlays trace the space of the access, both inside and out.

Again, the access overlays of the two case studies illustrate the differences between volumetric settings and fabrics. In Levittown, access is seen as a link between two points that need to be joined (figure 54, page 60). To minimize construction cost, the design focuses on minimizing square footage dedicated to movement. Therefore, the entry is part of the living area. One passes through the living room to enter the kitchen, the bedrooms, or the bath. The hallway is very short, just long enough to provide passage to the bedrooms, the bath, and a closet. Connection from the street to the front door is a path from some point on the sidewalk or drive to the stoop at the front door. A side door links vehicular and service access to the kitchen. Because of the focus on access solely as programmatic linkage, spaces not defined in the program become inaccessible. Thus, to use the back yards of early Levittown houses, one had to exit through the front or side of the house and pass through the side yard to reach the rear.

In the Sachs Apartments, the position, configuration, and dimensions of the access organize the setting (figure 55, page 61). At the site level, access is positioned between buildings, with these spaces serving both as paths to collective entries and as buffers between dwelling units (figures 53a–c). Within the dwellings, the access moves perpendicular to the direction of entry and parallel to the contours of the hill. Through its position, the access organizes the long, deep spaces into primary and personal dimensions. The access is more than a path for movement—it is light and dark, narrow and wide, as well as gardens, courtyards, thresholds, and dining rooms. By structuring access throughout the setting, from inside to out, Rudolf Schindler weaves access as a shared, continuous experience.

53a, b, c. Moving through the Sachs Apartments.

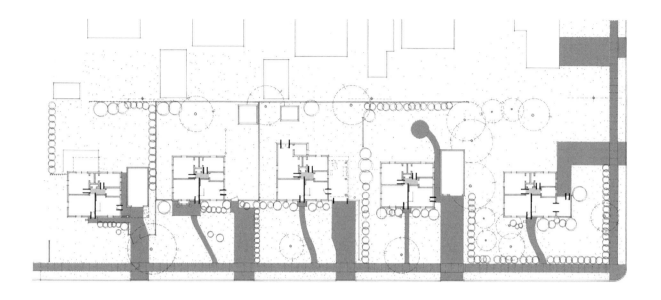

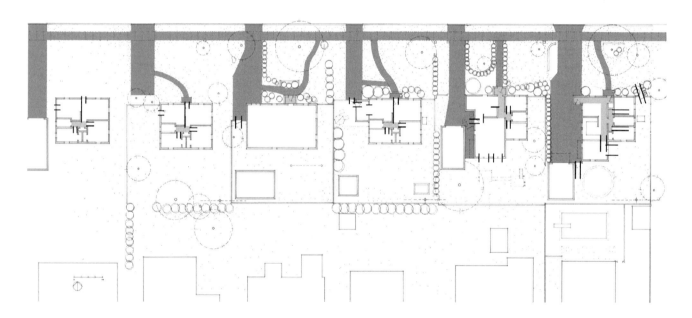

54. Levittown—accessed.

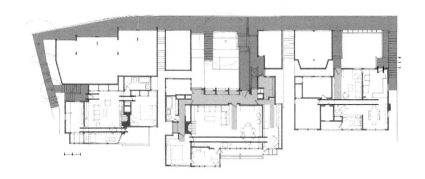

55. The Sachs Apartments—accessed.

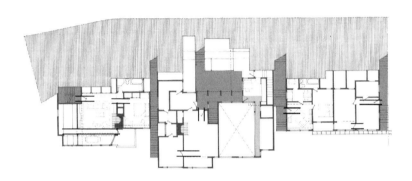

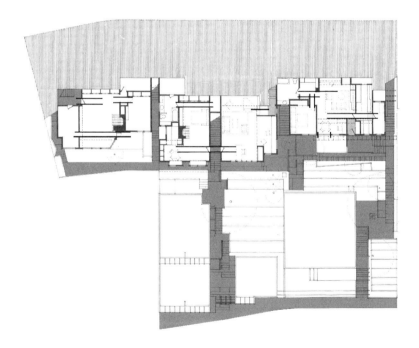

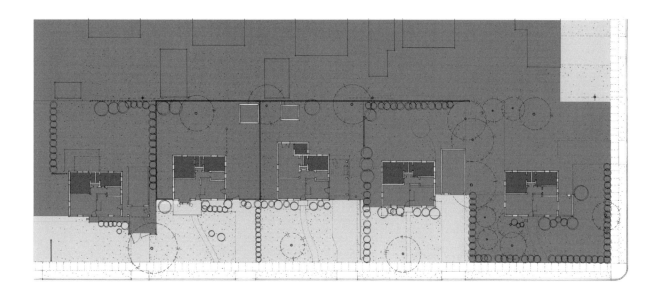

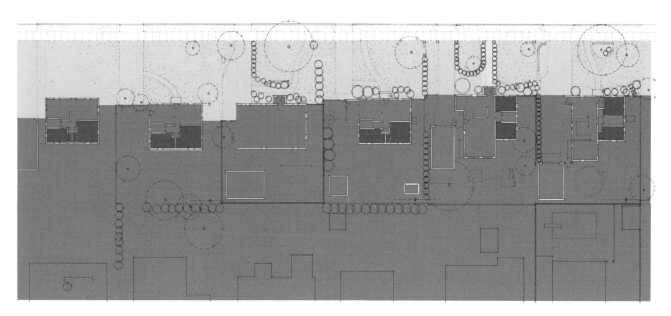

56. Levittown—claimed.

MAPPING CLAIM *Claim* is the control over territory and access that can be exerted by an individual or a group. In overlays that map claim, unshaded areas correspond to areas that are publicly claimed; light gray to areas claimed by neighbors; dark gray to areas claimed by a household; and black to areas claimed by an individual member of a household (figures 56 and 57).

This spectrum bridges changing perspectives of what constitutes public or private space as one moves within a setting. As described in the last chapter, a living area is private when viewed from the street because each household can limit access and use of the space to their invited guests. But the living area is public for those within the house because each household member can use the space and no one member controls it.

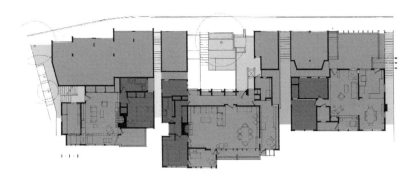

57. The Sachs Apartments—claimed.

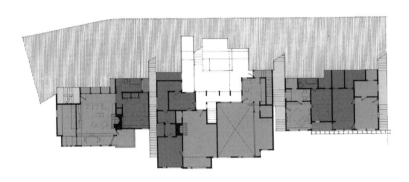

Although the terms *semipublic* and *semiprivate* also have been used to describe this shift in perspective, they still designate spaces as either public or private.

An overlay that maps claim is based on identifying the groups that can access and control any setting. "Public" territories are the spaces open to every individual—visitor, residents, and people just passing through. They are the spaces that can be accessed and used without infringing on another's control. Thus, as used in this book, *public* is not a comparative term but refers only to spaces that can be readily accessed by all individuals. Households that share physical proximity and have contiguous lots are *neighbors*, and their control of space is in response to their adjacency. *Household* refers to the spaces controlled by all the people living in a single dwelling unit, and *member* refers to a subgroup within a household—teens, grandparents, an au pair, a couple, or a single person—that uses a territory in exclusion of other household members or guests.

Although *community* does not appear as a claim group in these paired overlays, the term is used in other examples in this book. Here, it refers specifically to nonadjacent households that share spatially structured ways of dwelling that are not public. An example of a community claim is a golf course for the home owners of a particular association whose members do not all live adjacent to the golf course. This is a much narrower definition of community than the more common definition of the word, which evokes shared ways of living that are based on culture and traditions—for example, heritage, education, social standing, or political beliefs—that are not dependent upon physical adjacency.

Identifying the pertinent groups is a relative and critical exercise for the study of any setting. This particular set of groups is useful for a general rendering of claim in the suburbs, but the groups could change for each place and culture. Returning to the Herdeg example at Maidan-I-Shah, the groups there were identified as visitors, citizens, civil servants, clergy, and royalty. In a school, the groups might be students, faculty, staff, community members, and visitors. In households, grandparents or teens in extended families could be highlighted and separated for study. In this way, designers become aware of the spatial perceptions of different user groups.

In Levittown, the overlay (figure 56, page 62) reveals a pattern of layered claim dominated by the household. Moving perpendicular from the street into the depth of each block, one sees clear zones of transition from public to neighbor to a large area claimed by individual households.

The street, the sidewalk, and the strip of grass between the two can be publicly claimed. In this case, claim of a territory differs from ownership. Although individuals own the grass and sidewalk, these features are pro-

58. Continuous and collective neighborhood claim of front yards in Levittown.

59. Household claim of front yards on another street in Levittown.

vided to give the public access from one lot to another. The front yards of this setting (figure 58) form a continuous open space, filled with trees, cars, walks, drives, shrubs, plants, and lawn, collectively interpreted as a neighborhood zone. Again, the front yards are individually owned, but each house contributes to a pattern of claim in which fences and landscaping run parallel to the street and in a line with the front façade of the houses. Each household, consciously or not, sustains the neighborhood claim on the front yard. This pattern of neighborhood claim becomes more evident when compared with that of other settings in Levittown (figure 59) in which front yards are bounded by fences and plants that claim the yard for one household.

As first laid out, the claims on the Levittown setting were highly layered, from the neighborhood yard to a band of household-claimed spaces such as kitchens and living rooms to a band of bedrooms claimed by members (figure 60). And, as suggested earlier, the back yards were not accessible but were assumed to be claimed by the household. Over the last fifty years, this pattern has been transformed: the layering has been

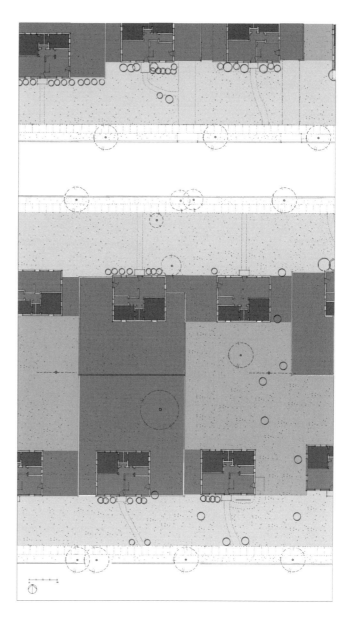

60. Levittown as claimed in 1957.

broken in ways that give household spaces connection to the rear yard. Thus, the spaces claimed by members are now interspersed in the fabric or have been moved to the second floor. The overall effect at the ground level is a setting that is uniformly claimed by household activities.

In the original settlement, this strict layering of increasingly individual use from the street to the rear of the house separated interior household activities from the exterior household spaces in the back yards. Over time, residents transformed this parallel set of layers so that spaces of household claim could be continuous from the house to the back yard. In some cases, the household claim is now continuous only with the back yard and is separated from the front yard. In other cases, the claim within the house has been turned 90 degrees so that household areas are connected to both the front and back yards.

chapter four

Unlike the transitioned banding of claim that parallels the streets of Levittown, the Sachs Apartments' overlay (figure 57, page 63) reveals a structure of spaces that are organized perpendicular to the streets and contours of the hill. These long spaces are alternately claimed as household or member spaces, with one unit's household space joined to the household space of another along a pedestrian path; member spaces adjoin other member spaces of the opposing neighbor, separated by a pedestrian path. In this way, each group in the setting—individuals, households, neighbors, and the public—has light and a view of the valleys and hill beyond (figures 61a–d).

61a, b, c, d. Views toward the landscape for all groups. *Top:* from the studio (member); *bottom left:* from an eating area (household); *bottom middle:* from the courtyard (neighbors); and *bottom right:* from the street (public).

seeing suburban dwelling as a fabric

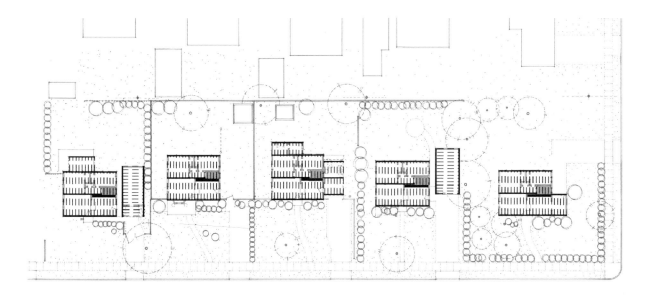

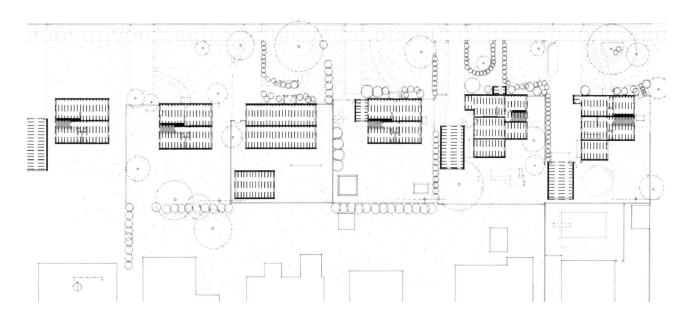

62. Levittown—assembled.

MAPPING ASSEMBLAGE *Assemblage* is the bringing together of material elements to form the spaces of our residential settings. This overlay studies building systems, in particular light wood frame construction, to highlight the relationship of assemblage to a setting.

The use of wood studs and joists characterizes light wood frame construction. Walls are typically assembled from 2 × 4– or 2 × 6–inch studs spaced 16 to 24 inches apart. These walls sit on a foundation and support upper floors and the roof. Gypsum wallboard—or plaster in older homes—is attached to the studs as interior finish. Sheets of plywood that resist lateral loads are nailed to the exterior of the wall studs, and the exterior finish may be wood or metal siding, brick facing, or stucco plaster. The floors are built of 2 × 10– or 2 × 12–inch joists spaced approximately

chapter four

63. The Sachs Apartments—assembled.

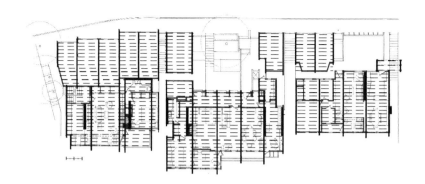

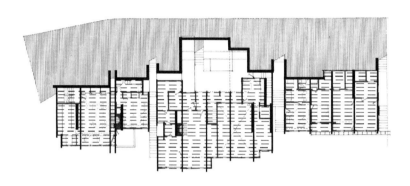

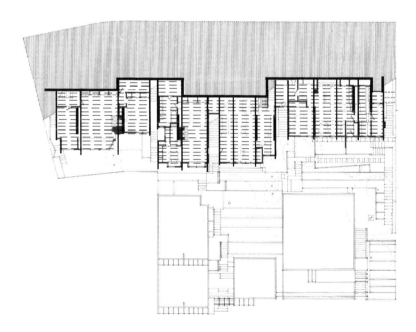

16 inches apart. Floor sheathing—either boards in older structures or plywood in newer buildings—is nailed to the top of the joists. A typical wood frame roof is constructed with 2 × 8– or 2 × 10–inch rafters, again spaced 16 to 24 inches apart. Roof sheathing, similar to floor sheathing, is nailed to the top of the rafters, and the roofing material (shingles, shakes, tiles, or built-up roofing) is applied to the top of the sheathing.

The components of light wood frame construction are readily assembled into a wide range of house forms and styles. Wood framing is employed by large-scale contractors as well as weekend hobbyists, in new construction as well as in renovation. For ease of layout and construction, the system has evolved so that all components have equal potential in any assembly. For example, the assembly of studs for a load-bearing wall is identical to that for a nonstructural wall. Plumbing, insulation, and ducts are sized to fit between the studs. Therefore, the same assembly can be used throughout a house, regardless of differences in the components' roles within the system. This development of a uniform construction system has led to practices that no longer distinguish between different actions in the framing system. Unfortunately, this ease in layout eliminates opportunities to design permeability in residential settings.

Light wood framing has two distinct structural roles—load-bearing and non-load-bearing. Bearing walls carry loads from the house to the foundation. To build an opening in these walls, headers or beams are added into the wall framing to transfer loads around the door, window, or passage. Therefore, load-bearing walls have a propensity to be more solid. Service and plumbing walls also are solid; they hold the pipes and major house equipment that are usually hidden from view. As their name implies, nonbearing walls do not carry load but are added to complete spatial enclosures and definitions. Openings, as well as any changes and modifications, are built more readily in nonstructural walls.

Overlays that map assemblage, such as those in figures 62 and 63 (see pages 68–69), highlight the differences between actions of the framing system to study the potential of assemblage in the life of a setting. Load-bearing walls are drawn as solid, bold lines, and the spanning of supported joists, rafters, or trusses is drawn as dotted (overhead) lines.[20] Likewise, solid, bold lines—slightly wider than the wall designation—highlight walls that contain primary services (plumbing, heating, and air conditioning). This overlay then intentionally renders the residential setting in such a way that the differences in the structural and mechanical actions in the system are highlighted. The bold walls are seen as infrastructural (more difficult and expensive to change) as well as solid (more difficult to open broadly without major changes to the construction system).

In the original Levitt houses (figure 62, page 68), the load-bearing framing and services all ran parallel to the street, in a direction that reinforced

chapter four

the separations in claim from neighbor to household to member spaces. The nonstructural gable ends faced neighboring houses, so the end walls were built solidly for privacy, in the same way as the load-bearing walls. This resulted in a uniform stud wall around the entire perimeter of each house where connections were reduced to small windows punctured in both load-bearing and nonbearing façades. Over time, many houses have expanded in the gable direction to the limits of the setback, but the net effect only relocates the solid gable end closer to a lot line (figures 64a–c).

64a, b, c. Growth of the Levitt homes in the nonstructural direction.

65. Sachs Apartments nonbearing façade.

The Levittown house is assembled of four separating walls at the perimeter of the house, and its assemblage reinforces the disconnection between inside and outside. This construction system builds the boxes that are characteristic of a volumetric setting.

In the Sachs Apartments overlay (figure 63, page 69), the representation reveals a load-bearing and service assemblage that builds a spatial orientation that is perpendicular to the contours and connects the dwelling units to the light and views of the landscape. The exterior, load-bearing walls are predominantly solid with openings punched into the surface. The exterior, nonbearing walls of the façades are assembled as screens with the wood frame construction expressed on the façade (figure 65). This façade has either a single screen layer that is dominated by window openings or a double layer of screens that form balconies and bay windows. The interior, nonstructural definitions are often just shelves or built-in furniture. The assembly of walls in the Sachs Apartments not only builds each apartment but also reinforces both the direction of connection to the landscape and the separation from adjacent neighbors.

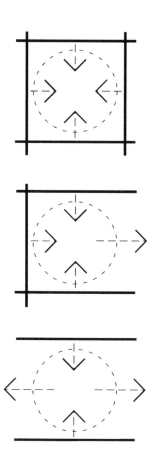

66. Diagrams of *(top to bottom)* complete, partial, and directionally contained spaces.

MAPPING CONTAINMENT   *Containment* describes how material elements hold and indicate spaces. This last overlay highlights the forms and organization of the material elements that define, limit, or bound the activity areas of dwelling. Although containment and assemblage can overlap in their spatial definition, they also have the potential to be independent of each other.

Of the five overlays, containment is the most concerned with describing the physical definitions of a setting. It suggests the spatial structuring of dwelling and establishes the territories within it. The physical definitions of containment can be complete, partial, or directional (as diagrammed in figure 66). A completely contained space is one in which materials border the full extent of the territory—it is a space that is defined at its perimeter. A space in which some of the boundaries are implied rather than delimited is partially contained.[21] Such spaces are both centered and directionally oriented toward the opening in the containment. Directionally contained spaces are defined by elements that are structured in parallel with each other. Containment is suggested through the reading of the frontal quality of the plane, and spatial connection is implied in the direction of extension of the parallel planes.

In overlays that map containment, such as those in figures 67 and 68, the material elements of containment are highlighted with solid, bold lines, and alignments and correspondence between forms of containment are rendered with thin lines. In this way, settings can hold both separations and connections.

When this depiction is applied to the early phase of Levittown settlement, complete containment dominates the definition of all the interior spaces at the room level as well as at the house level (figure 67). The exterior spaces are not defined or contained, but they are amorphous; this is made especially apparent by the slight shifts in the positions of the houses that emphasize each house as an object. Most contemporary housing is similarly contained at the room and house level. Although the houses appear to be less boxlike due to their highly articulated forms, the spaces are still completely contained, just aggregated into more complex boxes. This dominance of containment, particularly at the house level, is characteristic of volumetric settings.

In the Sachs Apartments, there is a directional structuring of walls with small returns (figure 68). The walls run perpendicular to the hill, generating interior and exterior spaces that are oriented toward the hill as well as directed out toward the landscape. In this setting, the containing walls structure relations between claims, and their extended direction builds connection to the larger landscape. When compared to the other overlays of the Sachs Apartments, the containment is very similar to the assemblage, with the exception of a 2-foot return at the ends of some walls

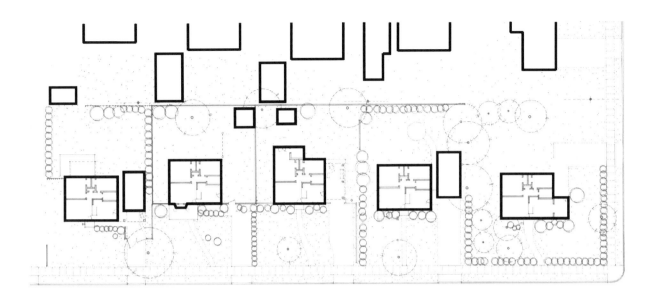

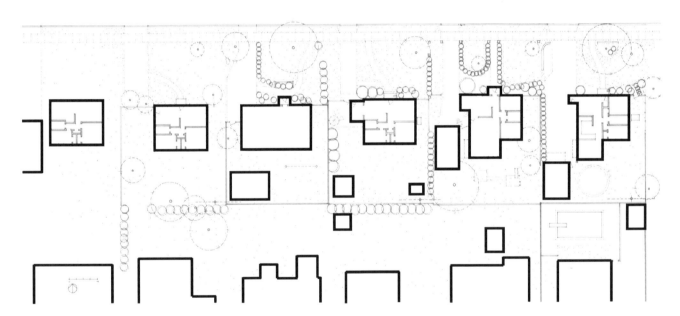

67. Levittown—contained.

68. The Sachs Apartments—contained.

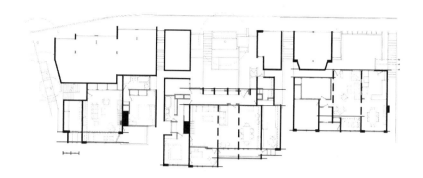

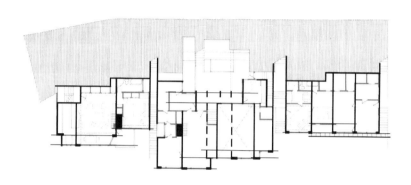

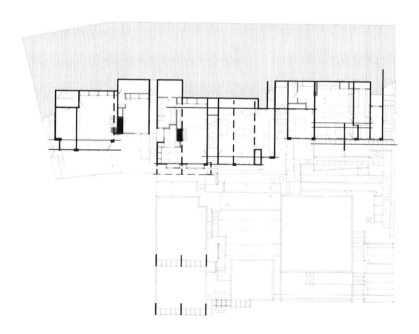

69a, b. Wall returns on the façade of the Sachs Apartments.

(figures 69a–b). The returns correspond with interior zones that were highlighted in the dimensional overlay. Thus, the dimensions for personal activities are not just added to a space but defined in the setting—from the exterior façade into interior fireplaces, built-in shelves, and lighting.

When the Levittown overlays are compared, the containment and the assemblage reveal very different structuring. The form of containment dominates the assemblage through the undifferentiated use of light wood framing. The containment overlay is more similar to the dimensional overlay, indicating a correspondence of single-use spaces with completely contained spaces.

What becomes apparent through comparative study of these two settings, as well as others that are described later in this book, is that those suburban settings that suffer most from interstitial waste, isolation, and ossification have distinct breaks in all the studied attributes at the boundaries of the houses. In the extreme, the attributes change position, organization, or definition at the perimeter of each house, highlighting the importance of the houses' shells and the settings' volumetric characteristics. In fabrics, the attributes are structured from house to house as well as from interior to exterior across a lot and into the broader setting. In volumetric settings, design emphasis is placed on the building, independent of the context; in fabrics, buildings are seen as components and contributors to the building of the context.

To return to the assessment of representation for design, the other limitation to experiential approaches is the nature of frames to isolate a portion of a fabric—there is always more information that lies beyond the border of the representation. Even with extensive experiential documentation of entire city fabrics and with new computational capabilities for lateral and zoom views, in every view some portion of the fabric is separated from its larger setting. In the process of design, what is not seen is often omitted from consideration.

Therefore, using experiential approaches to representation should be seen as an additional design approach, not *the* design approach. Any representation should be seen as a critical position toward the environment, not as a design method—for no one method is comprehensive enough or particular enough to engage the complexity of the environment. What the above narrative highlights is the confusion, among designers, between hierarchy as a phenomenon of levels or scales in an environment and hierarchy as a device to bring structure and organization to the environment. Designers need to be conscious of the arguments embedded in their design tools and to be fluent in a variety of representations to bridge the gaps in information that the use of any set of tools will entail. Competence in the design of continuities and connections for weaving fabrics is a necessary complement to the design of buildings themselves. In the particular case of the suburbs, making the design representation of places an explicit experiential exercise allows the task of housing design to move beyond the house, with a greater responsibility toward the setting.

[Some] appear to think more "holistically," paying greater attention to context and relationship, relying more on experience-based knowledge than abstract logic and showing more tolerance for contradiction. [Others] are more "analytic" in their thinking, tending to detach objects from their context, to avoid contradictions and to rely more heavily on formal logic.

Overall, Japanese subjects in the study made 70 percent more statements about aspects of the background environment than Americans, and twice as many statements about the relationship between animate and inanimate objects. A Japanese subject might note, for example, that "[t]he big fish swam past the gray seaweed."

"Americans were much more likely to zero in on the biggest fish, the brightest object, the fish moving the fastest," Dr. Nisbett said. "That's where the money is as far as they're concerned."

ERICA GOODE
"How Culture Molds Habits of Thought,"
New York Times (August 8, 2000), D1

part two | designing fabrics for dwelling

COMPRISING FOUR CHAPTERS, THE SECOND PART OF THIS BOOK EXPLORES THE POTENTIAL FOR DWELLING WHEN suburbs are developed as fabrics. While the first part describes how criticisms of the suburbs—their intransigence toward demographic and cultural change, their isolation and waste—arise because contemporary suburbs are mostly built volumetrically, the second part proposes and illustrates how designing dwelling as fabrics can address these criticisms.

Chapter 5, "Accommodating Choice," discusses demographic change and diversity in nonprogrammatic ways. It introduces the concept of capacity and describes how capacity in a setting promotes diversity in ways of living by increasing the potential for resident choice. Chapter 6, "Sharing in a Setting," describes the necessity for territorial sharing to support a sense of neighboring, not only as a shared image or infrastructure but also as individuals' contributions to a collective way of living. Chapter 7, "Unpacking," extends the discussion of neighboring to the physical construction of connections and separations in fabrics. By considering the containment of space as part of the formal structuring of a setting, we make continuity and permeability integral to a setting, without forsaking either privacy or autonomy. The last chapter, "Designing Density," argues for increasing density through morphology, not just quantity—through the design of the shared structure of a setting rather than the packing of functional activities. It demonstrates how embedding depth in the setting increases the transformational potential and variety needed for denser suburbs.

chapter five | accommodating choice

of living, accommodating diversity is a prime concern. The issue is no longer conformity but rather the mismatch between the suburban housing stock and social and demographic shifts in household composition. As in the exhibit "House Rules,"[1] their questioning typically begins with a recognition of the need to reconstitute our traditional image of a household: one mother, one father, 2.5 children, and a dog. As exhibit curator Mark Robbins asked, "Can the suburban house be reprogrammed to acknowledge and reflect social change?"[2]

The traditional image of a household is being challenged in light of a pluralistic reality. Yet Robbins's question inadvertently, but not atypically, points to continuing formulaic approaches to housing ways of dwelling. Dwelling should not be solved by "reprogramming"—defining "new" households and their lifestyles—because ways of dwelling are too great in number and are continually changing. As described in chapter 3, the complexity of dwelling arises from the multiplicity of ways in which we associate with a national culture, as well as with a variety of subgroups—ethnic, racial, religious, regional, occupational, economic, and life stage. It is accentuated by increasing acceptance of ways in which households are constituted: extended families, singles, nonrelated singles, single parents, and so on. Defining lifestyles is further complicated by the fluid ways in which we can change both our associations with these subcultures and our household compositions over time. Accommodating changing lifestyles by differentiating between and then designing for the particular patterns that emerge is an impossible task.

Nonetheless, contemporary housing development is obsessed with identifying lifestyles. Its goal, though, is to define normative descriptions that appeal to the broadest markets possible, with differences in ways of living seen as variations on the norms. To provide options in housing, developers solve the problem of diverse and changing lifestyles through providing a variety of model homes—thus supplying a consumer's choice. This approach limits housing configurations and capitalizes upon the ability of people and households to adapt. More significantly, it views the dialogue of dwelling as static rather than temporal, limiting everyday and longer-term choices.

An alternative view presumes that dwelling, if allowed to do so, will find its place. The task of dwelling design is not to prescribe a fit between a lifestyle's activities and a house's form but to design housing to support a range of interpretations in the readings and uses of forms. This requires studying habitation as a continuous expression of choice. For instance, where could each person sleep? How do people sleep—all together or separately? On what can they sleep? What other activities accompany sleeping? Will guests come into the sleeping area? Could one sleep in the front of the house or the back, at grade level or above? Where could a guest or new family member sleep? Residents continually make choices and changes by assessing their ways of living in relation to their setting. Our job is to design for choices rather than to make prototypes to choose from.

stories of choice

Each household's way of dwelling tells a story. The dialogue of that story is an exchange between how a household chooses to live and how it reads its setting. People develop a correspondence between the ways they live and the spaces of a setting through choices that express their lifestyles.[3] Residents project their lifestyle by associating with and occupying the nooks and corners, walls and windows, rooms, houses, yards, and neighborhood. Two stories follow. One is from the city of San Francisco and the other from an outlying San Francisco suburb.

Leo Lopez[4] owns a San Francisco Victorian that was subdivided into six dwelling units. Of the units, he selected the second-floor front unit as most suitable for his lifestyle. Leo, once married, is now an avowed bachelor with a grown son who visits every weekend. When together, Leo and his son mostly eat out, but they enjoy entertaining and watching television at home. At first glance, the unit Leo chose would seem most readily occupied as a one-bedroom apartment (figures 70a–b). Typically, entertaining, dining, and food preparation activities would occupy the front, middle, and back rooms, respectively, with a bedroom off the front entertaining area. Yet Leo needs two sleeping areas, since he and his son do not want to share a room.

Leo reads the space of his apartment in a way that makes it similar to

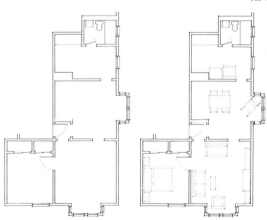

70a, b. Leo's apartment—empty *(left)* and occupied as a one-bedroom unit *(right)*.

71. *Near right:* Leo's childhood home in Guadalajara, Mexico.

72. *Far right:* Leo's apartment—Leo's reading of the unit for two sleeping areas.

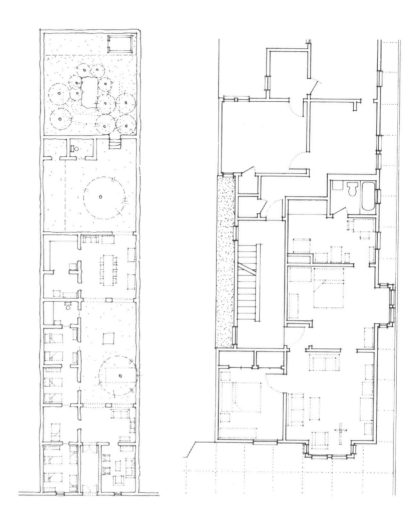

his childhood courtyard house in Guadalajara (figure 71). In that house, all the activities and rooms were organized around a central outdoor courtyard. Although no assigned activity occurred in the courtyard itself, it was the center around which daily activities took place. Rooms used for sleeping, dining, entertaining, and cooking were all accessed through the courtyard, with an internal route implied by door openings between rooms. Several family members occupied each *recamara*, using the rooms for sleeping as well as entertaining.

Although Leo's current home does not have an outdoor courtyard, he locates his television/entertainment activities in the front room, with two *recamaras* surrounding it. Although others may use this unit as a linear, one-bedroom apartment, Leo reads and occupies his space as a centrally organized, two-*recamara* dwelling (figure 72).[5]

Our second story is about the Changs,[6] who purchased a house outside San Francisco (figure 73). At most times of the day, the wife, the husband, and their five-year-old son prefer to be together in a room, although they are often engaged in separate activities. As a result, several rooms hold

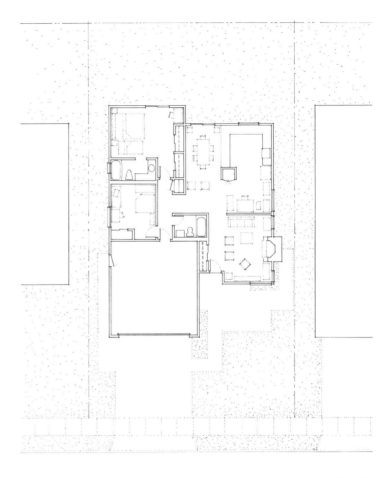

73. The Changs' choices.

similar furnishings: whether a room is a bedroom, living room, or kitchen, it has books and toys for the son as well as tables and shelves for the parents. The room designated as their son's bedroom is rarely used, except as a guest room. Instead, the family sleeps together in one room, using a small trundle bed for the boy.

The Changs feel that the house suits them well, complaining only about the fireplace and dining room. They would have preferred a house without a fireplace because for them it has associations with dirt, cold, and smoke, not hearth and warmth. Nonetheless, they take advantage of the fireplace's focal location by placing their wide-screen television on the hearth. As for the dining room, it is too narrow to hold a round table with a lazy Susan on it. Instead, the Changs had to buy a rectangular table. Now, when hosting a dinner party, they must pass dishes to their guests rather than serve them directly.

The dialogue in these stories is not predetermined—a form in the physical setting is not coupled with a specific pattern of living, just as a change in function does not always require an altering of form. At the same time, where we live is not independent of how we live—the form of a place is not irrelevant to its inhabitation. These two homes illustrate the ways in which design addresses dwelling. The Changs' house, designed to

chapter five

meet a particular lifestyle, supports a limited range of choices; the Changs both impose and modify their way of living to make the house suit their needs. Leo Lopez's home, typical of many San Francisco houses, accommodates a wider range of interpretations. Functional approaches to housing American diversity limit choice making by residents because ways of living are assumed to be specific and static. For the Changs, this does not necessarily make them live as prescribed, but it limits—and sometimes frustrates—how they want to live.

To better accommodate stories of dwelling like that of Leo Lopez, designers need to embed the potential, or the capacity, in a setting for residents to make more choices about the ways in which they live. Looking at the systems that contribute to the dialogue of dwelling reveals why some residential settings limit stories to fit a theme while others more comfortably accommodate the uniqueness of each story.

capacity in the fabric

San Francisco is home to many diverse lifestyles, spread throughout the city in a relatively homogeneous housing stock. Although there are districts associated with particular ethnicities or cultures, they are not settled in exclusion of other groups. Also, cultural associations with particular districts shift over time. Outside the city, in Clayton, is a community whose housing shares many physical characteristics with San Francisco, yet the ways in which the residents choose to live seem more homogeneous. Are the similarities in Clayton and the differences in San Francisco just circumstances of history or urbanity, or does the form of the setting contribute?

74. *Top:* Clayton, California.

75. *Bottom:* San Francisco, California.

Houses in both communities are built on narrow lots, with the short ends of the houses facing the street. In each setting, the houses are positioned so that there is a front yard, a back yard, and side yards, with parking in front. In Clayton (figure 74), the lots are 40 feet wide by 120 feet deep, with a 25-foot front yard setback and 5-foot side yard setbacks. Parking is at grade. The predominant orientation of the interior spaces is toward the private rear yard, although windows also face the side yards for light and ventilation. In San Francisco (figure 75), a block is subdivided into lots that are typically 25 feet to 27.5 feet wide by 140 feet deep. On each lot is a house that has a front yard setback of about 12 feet and side yard setbacks of about 3.5 feet. Parking, if available on site, sits half a level below the street and under the front portion of the house. Interior spaces are oriented for light and ventilation toward either the street or the private space at the rear of the lot.

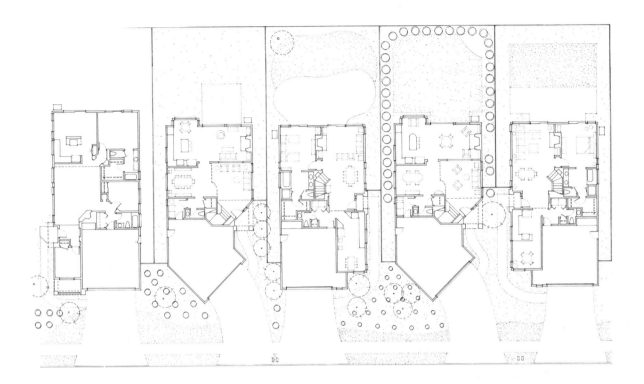

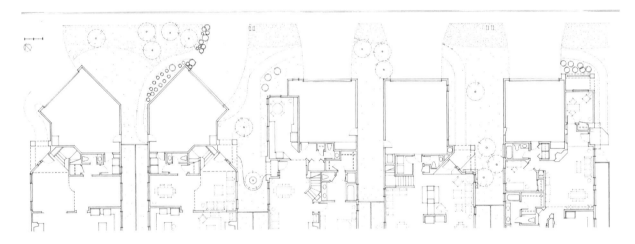

76. Clayton—inhabited.

These two case studies exemplify different formal paradigms for accommodating choice: in Clayton (figure 76), a functional programming of lifestyles that limits ways of living by seeing dwelling as static; and in San Francisco (figure 77), the embedding of a fabric with capacity to house multiple and changing ways of living. Although the houses in each setting were developed to accommodate the lifestyles of their time, the San Francisco houses have absorbed many new ways of living that Clayton's functionally efficient, post–World War II houses have not.

chapter five

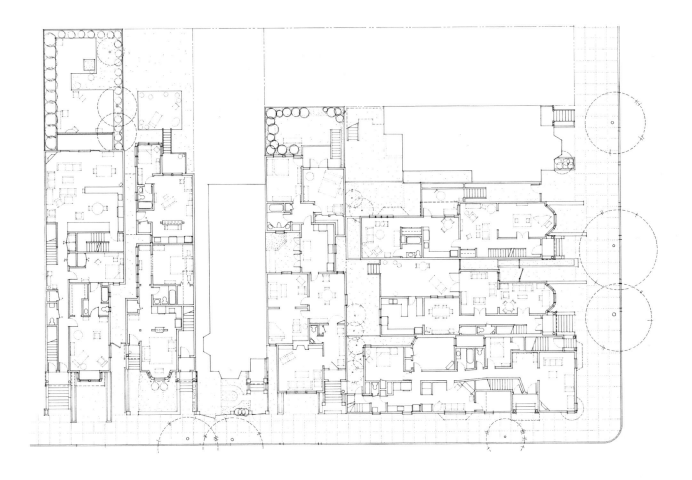

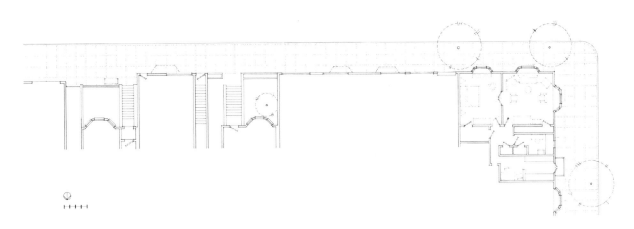

77. San Francisco—inhabited.

In Clayton, the general choice, location, and layout of the activities within each house are predictable. Typically, the only variations in choices made by households that occupy the same model home are in the kind and arrangement of furniture selected. In San Francisco, the choices of habitation are not always predictable despite the similarity of plan from house to house. The difference is in the capacity of the San Francisco fabric to be read in a range of ways.

Capacity in housing should not be confused with its programming, the specification of the activities of a lifestyle. A program states that a "breakfast nook" is required that has a certain area or dimension to hold a certain number of people. Capacity, in contrast, is the ability of the spatial form of the setting—through its configurations, dimensions, and positions—to contain or suggest a variety of uses. Capacity supports inhabitational readings or interpretations of the dwelling environment without necessitating architectural changes in the short term. It can also support adaptational choices by suggesting how physical changes can be made in the long term. It extends the functional requirements of a program by holding multiple configurations of inhabitation and receiving multiple associations. For example, a bay window at the edge of a living area defines a territory for individual activities within the larger room of the household. It can hold a seat, a table, a work area, or a "breakfast nook," as selected by the resident.

The concept of capacity, though broadly used and understood,[7] needs to be further described to be useful for design. A systemic study of the case studies reveals how a fabric can be embedded with capacity that increases a house's ability to accommodate choice. Four attributes prove influential: *access*—how people move through a house; *claim*—how people establish control over a space; *dimension*—the structure of the sizes of activity spaces; and *assemblage*—the structural and service infrastructure of dwelling.

CAPACITY IN ACCESS   As defined in chapter 4, access provides ways of moving between, into, and through spaces; it is a spatial connection between activities within a setting.[8] As such, access organizes space for use. For example, if a space is accessed at its edge, the area is most commonly read as a single territory. If a space is accessed at its center, the area can be read as a single space or as two equal territories separated by the access. If the space is accessed at another point—for instance, 2 feet from an edge—again the area can be read as a single space or as two unequal territories, a larger one for a primary use and a 2-foot zone that holds personal choices for use. The simple positioning of access can change the capacity of a room, house, or neighborhood for choice (figure 78).

In Clayton and San Francisco, the overall patterns of access are similar

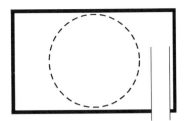

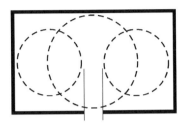

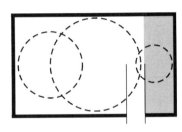

78. The position of access generates capacity.

(figures 79 and 80). To reach the house, one turns 90 degrees away from the public sidewalk and street, moves through the front yard, and then goes into the house. Proceeding through the house, one moves through the interior areas, eventually reaching an outdoor space at the rear of the lot. Beyond this general progression from a public front to a private back, the presentation of choice to residents is quite different.

To enter a house in Clayton, one first must walk on the driveway and then onto a path that leads around the garage to the front door. This is the one public entry from the street, although a resident may opt to enter through the garage. In the San Francisco setting, there are many ways to enter the houses—front or side, ground or first level—that either were originally built as variations on a type or have evolved over time. The typical entry sequence is to move from the sidewalk onto a path that leads directly to stairs that go up half a story to an entry porch. This entire sequence occurs in a zone to one side of the house's front yard. Another entry sequence provides access along the side of the house to reach the rear yard or accessory units in houses that have been subdivided. Between these two is an entry half a story below grade or at grade that provides access to a level below a plinth. This level has been commonly transformed to hold commercial, parking, rental, or office spaces. By accommodating many possibilities for entry, each house has the potential to operate as a single unit or multiple units, for single or multiple use.

After one passes through the entry, the reading of choice again differs between the two settings. In Clayton, the access can be characterized as a path, either linear or circular, that provides a way to reach all the activities. Despite an open plan without halls, the circulation through spaces is clearly implied as a route to and from activity areas. The implied access is located at the edge of most of the activity spaces, maximizing the area for a specified activity and minimizing the potential for other activities or choices.

In San Francisco, the access is both dimensioned and positioned to increase interpretations for use. The primary access within the house is clearly delineated in the form of a hallway, especially in the front half of the house, that provides access to rooms along its length. This hallway is typically positioned 3 to 4 feet away from the exterior wall that runs the depth of the lot. As in the example of the room, this position of the hall organizes the primary activities on one side of the house and service and personal activities in a 3- to 4-foot zone on the other side of the access. Not only does this zone hold physical changes such as half-baths, closets, and stairs, it also increases the hall's capacity for day-to-day choices. In some houses, the passageway holds a sideboard and seats; in others, it serves as an entry hall or even a dining area.

Unlike the Clayton houses, which have a single path, some of the San

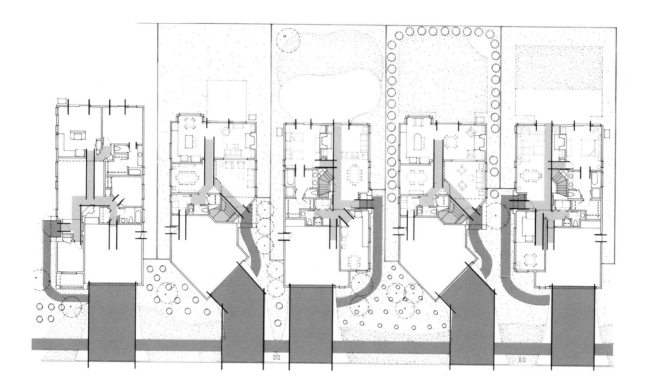

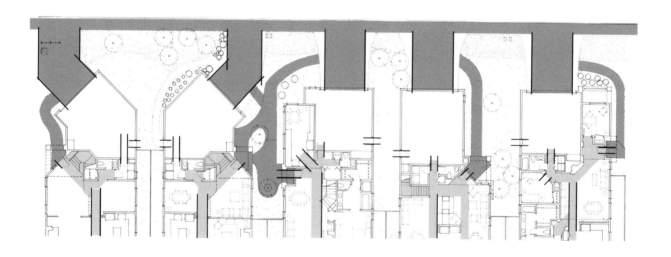

79. Clayton—accessed.

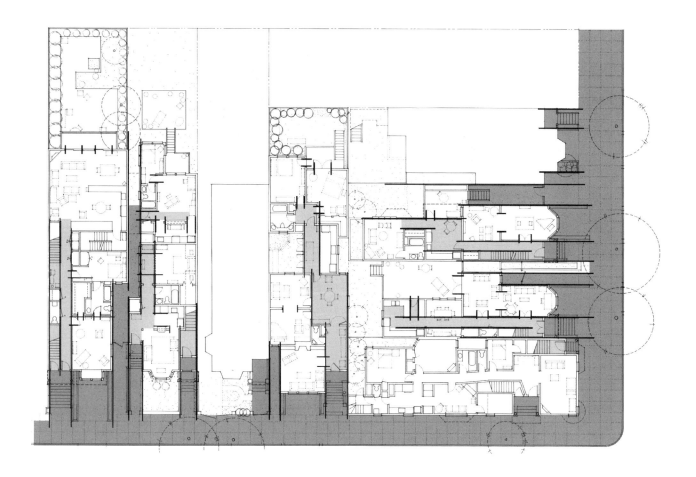

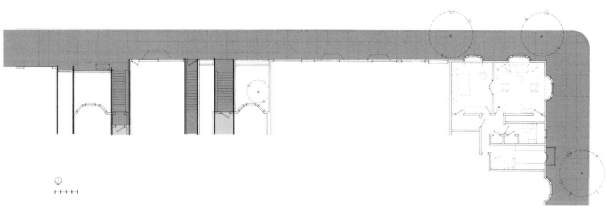

80. San Francisco—accessed.

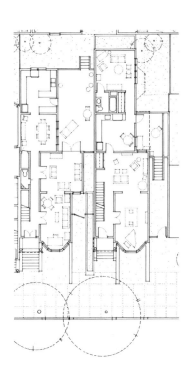

81. Occupation of the front rooms in San Francisco.

Francisco houses have another parallel access independent of the hallway. For instance, the front room is connected with an adjacent room—originally the "double parlor"—through a 4- to 6-foot-wide opening. The decision to allow movement between these rooms is made by residents depending on their reading of the spaces and their lifestyle needs. It is possible because access to activities deeper in the lot is already provided by the hall. The choice made can be seen in residents' furniture arrangements (figure 81). The residents in the house on the left chose to block access between the front and second rooms; the residents in the middle house chose to connect the two rooms. In the house on the right, the household, which was composed of three unrelated people, chose to make the three front rooms individual—closing the doors between the two front parlors and arranging the furniture as if there were no opening.

The lesson here is not that hallways provide choice. There are many examples of dreary hallways that do not offer much option other than to move through them as quickly as possible. The lesson is that embedding capacity in the organization, dimension, and form of access allows a setting to be inhabited by residents to suit their changing needs.

CAPACITY IN CLAIM   *Claim* is the control over a territory or access that can be exerted by an individual or a group.[9] As a guest in a house, a person may be able to move into an area, yet the form of the access—whether a door is ajar or closed, the nature of the threshold to a passageway, the quality of light at the end of the hall—is read as an indication of whether to go farther. Likewise, if residents want to indicate their claim over a space, they accentuate their control—by opening or closing curtains, doors, or gates, by turning on a light, or by positioning certain activities next to each other—in order to exclude or welcome. The ways that people both claim territories and read claims are informed by past experiences. As before, the question is how house form enables interpretations of claim.

In Clayton, households that live in the same model of home exhibit the same patterns of claim (figure 82). The open plan of the living, dining, and cooking areas excludes private activities from those parts of the house. Likewise, member spaces are smaller, cellular, and separated from the rest of the house to provide privacy, excluding shared household activities from those parts of the house. The form of the house suggests that sleeping is a private, individual, and isolated activity. Yet, for some people,

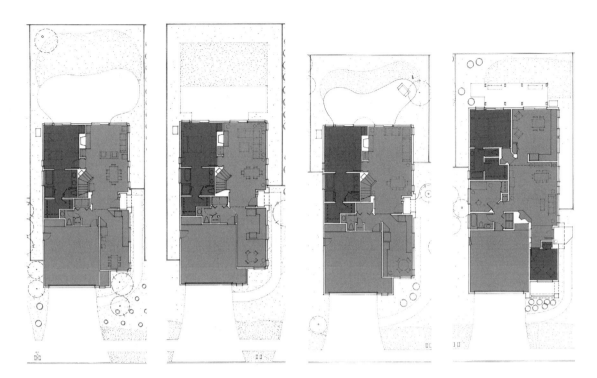

82. Residents of the same model of home claim them in similar ways.

sleeping areas can be shared spaces for family members and guests and do not require separation from the rest of the house, as in Leo Lopez's story. When these model homes are randomly distributed through individual home owner selection, claims become scrambled in the setting (figure 83). A territory claimed by a member of one household can sit next to an adjacent household's living room.

In the San Francisco houses, there is a public-to-private gradient of space from the street to the rear yard (figure 84). Because the rooms have similar sizes, shapes, and orientations, function is not the primary way to read a room. Although these rooms were built to accommodate particular activities of the early-twentieth-century family, current residents interpret the rooms' forms to suit their new requirements and claims. While one resident claims the front room as a living area overlooking the street, another household elects to place its living area at the back of the house, overlooking the yard.

The settings in both Clayton and San Francisco exhibit random patterns of claim in the setting, but there are important distinctions. Because the pattern is generated by resident choices in San Francisco, it is not static, as in Clayton, but is only a snapshot of an evolving sequence. As a consequence, should there be conflicts between household claims, one set of residents may choose to change their occupation of a space if they are uncomfortable with their relations to the setting. Also, the solid walls in the San Francisco setting are parallel with the depth of the site. As a result, openings between inside and outside face the front and rear yards,

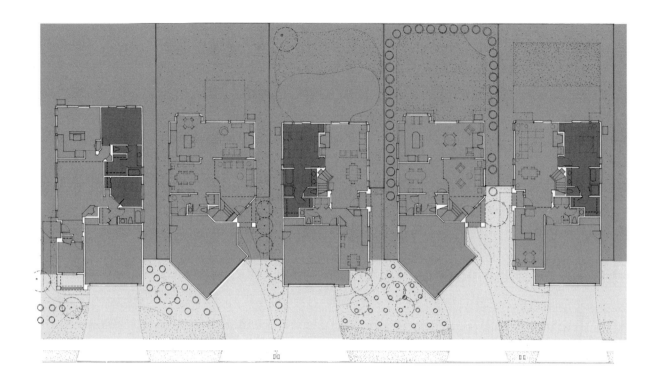

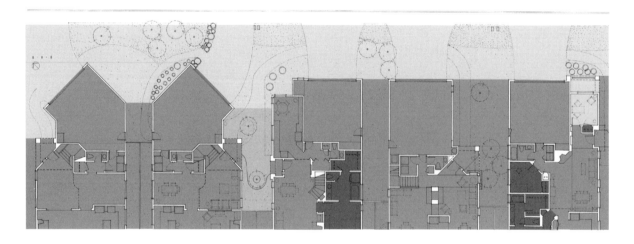

83. Clayton—claimed.

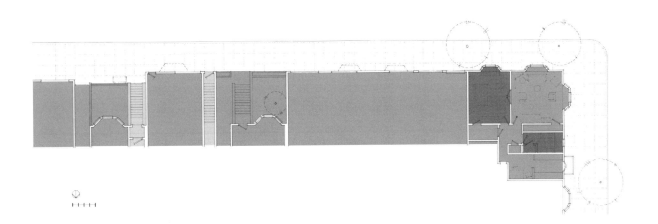

84. San Francisco—claimed.

territories of the same household. In Clayton, the windows open onto the side yards and thus look upon territories of other households.

The front exterior zone of the houses can also be studied for choices in claim. In both settings, the garage occupies a majority of the front width of the lot, leaving only enough dimension for access to an entry. In the Clayton development, positioning the garage at grade separates dwelling activities from the front yard. By default, not choice, the household is isolated from the street. In San Francisco, the garage is located half a level below the main level of the house, allowing a person above the garage area to look out upon the street, with privacy ensured by the change in level. A household can choose the degree of connection or separation that it makes with the street through its inhabitation of both the bay window and the front yard.

In this San Francisco neighborhood, there is a common way of inhabiting front yards: low curbs and shrubs demarcate the area of each household's claim while still inviting visitors into the house. This is a choice, shared by several residents, that is made more apparent when a household chooses not to welcome but to exclude uninvited pedestrians by erecting a 4-foot-high fence around the perimeter of its yard, as in figure 84, third house from the left, and in figure 85.

Again, the lesson for design is not to mimic San Francisco Victorians by making all rooms the same size and configuration but to avoid over-segmenting and specializing spaces for use or claim. Whether on a room-by-room basis or through a range of claims throughout the house, the form of a fabric can enable residents to make and, more important, remake the choice of claim.

CAPACITY IN DIMENSION   *Dimension* refers to the sizes of activity spaces and the organization of those sizes.[10] In the earlier example of the room with a bay window, the room's dimensions have a capacity to enable multiple readings. The room can be read as a single territory or as two territories—a large area that holds a primary activity such as entertaining, dining, or sleeping, as well as a smaller area, configured on one side by the bay window, that holds personal activities such as writing, reading, informal dining, or working. In this way, the room holds the potential to be read for one or for several activities simultaneously.

In the Clayton houses (figure 87, page 98), dimensions are laid out to fulfill a program. For each specified function, dimensions are determined on the basis of normative standards for the activity as well as its furnishings and equipment. When "efficiency" through minimal sizes is the objective, the number of possible configurations for an activity is intentionally limited. These dimensions are then arranged according to the program's adja-

85. San Francisco—one enclosed front yard.

cency requirements. The size and organization as well as fenestration reinforce a room's specificity of use as master bedroom, child's room, formal living room, and so on. Since the form of the house in Clayton is generated from a program of activities, unprogrammed interior space is intentionally eliminated. When dimension is tied solely to program, a resident's choices become more limited—typically to the kind of furniture and its arrangement within predetermined uses for each room. Introducing other uses, either primary or personal, can be frustrating.

In San Francisco (figure 88, page 99), dimensional analysis reveals bands of 6-foot zones arrayed through the depth of the site and 3- to 4-foot zones that parallel the access within the house. Sizes are not structured solely by function and adjacency; rather, these dimensions are also arrayed to increase capacity in the house and the setting. Residents' choices of habitation show at least two ways of reading these dimensional zones: one zone supports one activity, or combinations of zones hold an activity. It is also important to note the sizes of the zones: 3 feet, 6 feet, and then 10 to 12 feet. These sizes, whether alone or in combination, are compatible with a broad range of primary and personal activities; their particular use is left to the residents.

Although the houses in Clayton have significantly less dimensional capacity than the houses in San Francisco, they are not bereft of spaces for personal choice. In general, these homes have a generosity of overall dimension for each room as well as capacity for personalization around the fireplace core, an "entertainment center" of built-in cabinetry. One model home in Clayton has a front room that is intentionally left ambiguous for resident choice. It is programmed to be "unprogrammed"—its use is to be designated by the resident. When compared to the dimensional capacity within houses such as Levittown, both the primary and personal dimensions in Clayton houses are far more generous (figure 86, below).

86. Clayton *(left)* and Levittown *(right)*—house-level dimensional capacity.

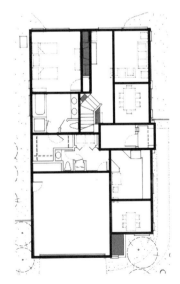
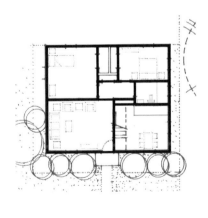

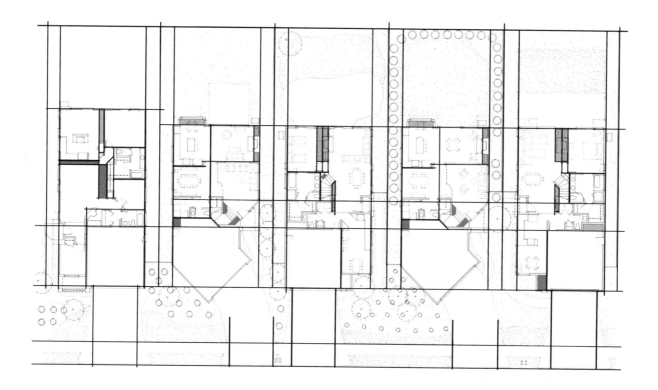

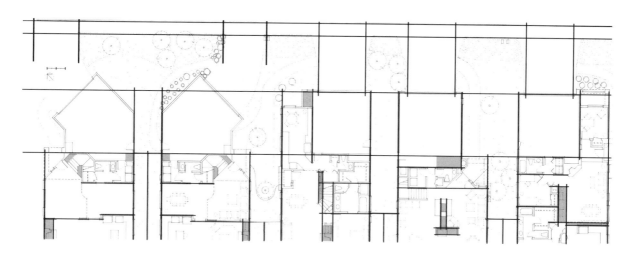

87. Clayton—dimensioned.

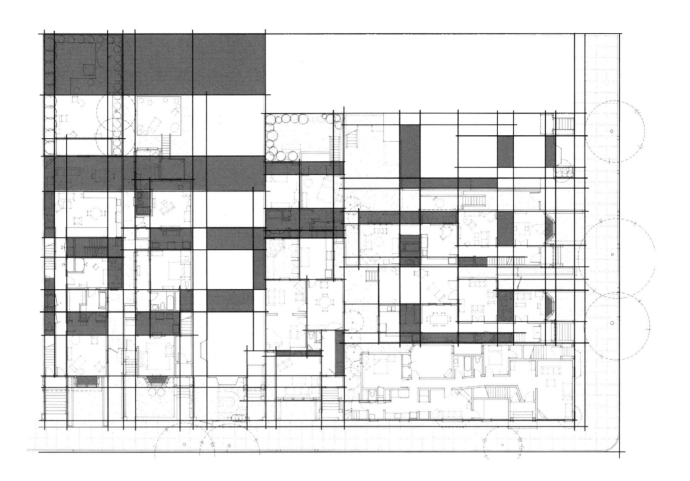

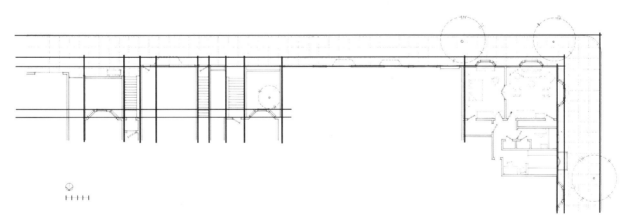

88. San Francisco—dimensioned.

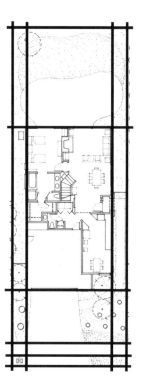

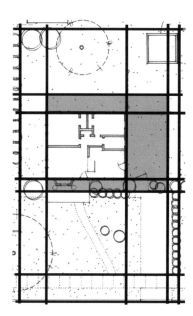

89. Clayton *(left)* and Levittown *(right)*—
site-level dimensional capacity.

At the level of the lot and neighborhood, the dimensional capacity of the setting is yet another story. Again, more accommodation of choice through dimensions is found in San Francisco than in Clayton. But Levittown is far more generous than Clayton (figure 89). Clayton is again typical of contemporary development in that the dimensions of the outdoor spaces continue to be programmatically determined and structured house by house. The front yard setback is just deep enough to accommodate the length of a car in front of a garage. The back yard is just long enough to hold an outdoor activity—for instance, play equipment or a patio with barbecue. At 5 feet wide, the side yards act as minimal buffers from the neighboring houses and provide fire access to the rear of the lot. Increased land and infrastructure costs, coupled with extensive programmatic expectations, lead to larger houses on smaller plots. Each model home is wrapped with the smallest possible apron of land that fulfills the defined outdoor activities, reinforcing the house-by-house ordering of dimensions and the volumetric characteristics of the setting. There is no dimension for extensions of the house at the ground level.

In San Francisco, the house's dimensional structuring is continuous between the inside and outside. The pattern previously described for the house, wide bands alternating with narrow ones, structures the entire lot and neighborhood. The front of the house has a 3-foot zone in which both interior and exterior spaces are positioned—mostly bay windows and front stair landings. In the rear of the houses, the alternation of sizes continues, but with a greater degree of variation in the zones' occupation.

Although Levittown is often used to caricature the suburbs, its capacity for choice at the site level is much greater than that of many contemporary suburbs such as Clayton. In Levittown, minimizing construction cost was more critical than minimizing land cost. As a result, the dimensional capacity of the houses is minimal, but the lots themselves are dimensionally generous by present-day standards. In Levittown, each house is positioned forward on the lot, toward the street and to one side, to accommodate car access at the other side of the house. As a result, this positioning generates a dimensional capacity in the site to one side of each house and at the rear. Over time, this dimension accommodates many extensions and additions and has supported a local building industry that specializes in enlarging the Levitt house.

Dimensional capacity addresses how a form is read as a cultural practice, not as a specification of a way of living. In Clayton, the dimensions are generated to fulfill a house's program. In San Francisco, the sizes and structure order the setting as a fabric into which programs can be read and reread, increasing the capacity and range of choices for residents.

CAPACITY IN ASSEMBLAGE   The use of building assemblies to increase choice is common practice. For instance, in the building code, light wood framed wall and flooring systems are oversized to obtain a structural capacity for uncommon static and active household loads and distributions. Thus, a large party, a waterbed, and a grand piano can occupy different parts of a house and need not be fixed to one corner of a particular room. Again, the design challenge is to ask in what ways assemblage can support a greater range of choice. And again, the case study overlays provide some alternatives.

In Clayton (figure 90), the structural assemblage is directed primarily toward forming rooms. The bearing walls and beams are multidirectional—both parallel and perpendicular to the lot lines—emphasizing the equivalence of the roles of the stud wall system over the structural differences. In San Francisco (figure 91), the assembly of load-bearing walls and the span of floor joists are directional, with the bearing walls running parallel to the side yard lot lines. Windows, doors, and partition walls infill between the bearing walls. Rather than being driven solely by room definitions, this structural assemblage also establishes connections to the setting—with light, between rooms, with the street and rear yard—as well as separation between adjacent neighbors.

The spatial structuring of the bearing and nonbearing assemblage embeds an adaptational capacity in the San Francisco assemblage. Although one of the advantages of wood framing is the malleability of the system, changing nonbearing walls has fewer ramifications for the support of the remainder of the house. In San Francisco, the 6-foot bands of

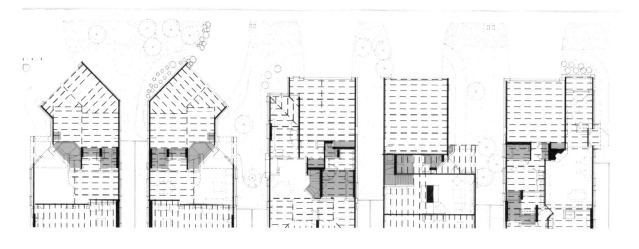

90. Clayton—assembled.

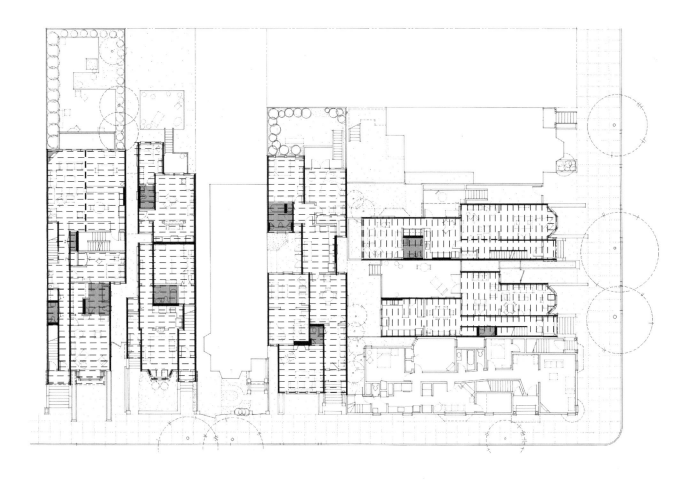

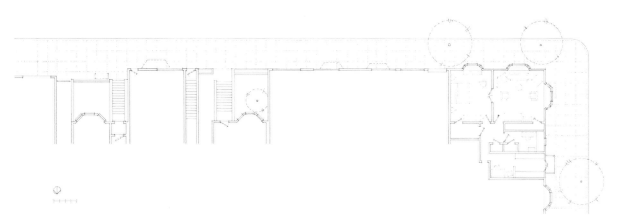

91. San Francisco—assembled.

92. Three elevations of the original Levittown model home.

dimensional capacity work in concert with the structural system. Renovations to change, incorporate, or separate the 6-foot zones are easily defined with nonbearing partition walls. In Clayton, each wall of a room either is bearing or contains servicing, limiting the potential for adaptations and emphasizing the interior of each room without relation to its setting.

Clear distinctions between load-bearing and non-load-bearing walls embed a different kind of potential for variation in the setting than the deployment of different model homes. The variation from house to house in Clayton is achieved by randomly deploying one of four model homes, with further variations achieved by mirroring house plans and substituting gabled with hipped roofs. In other developments, like the initial phase at Levittown (figure 92), there was only one prototype with different exteriors. In both cases, after initial construction, the variation in the setting is in the appearance of the houses, not in the choices of living.

In San Francisco, the initial variations in façades can be attributed to individual interpretations of a type, but the assemblage of the type builds a potential for choices and changes not found in Clayton. The bearing walls in San Francisco are mostly solid, with a few punched openings. They are largely uniform, wood-sided surfaces, and attention to detail focuses on the window openings. The nonbearing walls, however, are highly articulated and individualized, freed of the constraints of structural loads. To build these individualized façades, an industry evolved to manufacture components from which builders could craft a façade. Over time, residents could change these fronts. Some added entries as houses became apartments; some removed entries as apartments were converted into single-family homes; garage doors allowed cars to enter the houses at ground level; and storefronts changed some dwellings into mixed use (figure 93).

93. San Francisco—changes in the non-load-bearing façades.

The structure of service elements and the spaces they support can also affect a setting's capacity for choice. Because walls that contain primary ventilation, plumbing, or electrical services are more difficult to relocate, they, like the bearing walls, resist change. In Clayton (figure 90, page 102), the service spaces are aggregated to build a barrier between the house and garage, separating the household from the activities of the street.[11] These spaces' service walls tend to reinforce the multidirectional character of the structural assembly. The web of walls that surround the utility rooms ultimately limits choices. This buffer area is less likely to support change in either the use or the reconfiguration of the spaces.

A comparison with servicing structure in San Francisco (figure 91, page 103) shows how assembly enables choice. Typically, the service walls of San Francisco houses run parallel to but independent of the bearing walls. They reinforce the directions of the fabric. The service spaces occupy the space between the bearing and service wall, dimensionally limited between these two walls but with capacity to change in the non-bearing direction. Thus, this servicing arrangement has a potential to expand and contract.[12]

It is not only the form and direction of the services that enable choice but their position as well. A common practice in housing design is to broadly group dwelling activities into three areas: living and household activities; sleeping and individual activities; and service areas that include the kitchen, laundry, storage, and utilities (figure 94). Often, service areas

94. Area relationships as typically structured with services (Talcott et al. 1986).

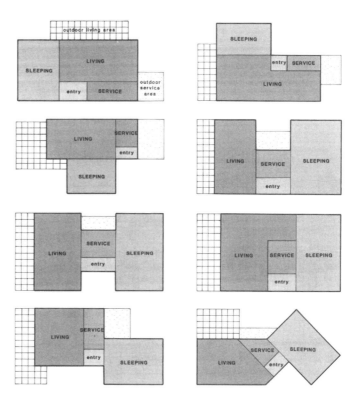

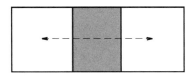

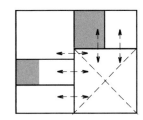

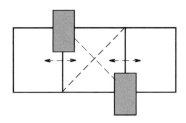

95. Capacity in the reading of access generated by the position of services (shaded).

are placed between living and sleeping areas to serve as a buffer between the active and passive activities of dwelling, as shown in the bottom four diagrams of figure 94. This configuration of live-service-sleep reinforces assumptions about sleeping as a private activity—a story that is not universal but culturally specific.

A live-service-sleep model for organizing a house is dependent upon a linear configuration of access to connect activities. Yet the patterns of dwelling for many Americans such as the Lopezes and the Changs evolved from living in courtyard houses with a concentrically based form of access.[13] A concentric organization gives nearly equal access to several rooms, de-emphasizing immediate specificity of use based on position in relation to access. Service spaces are linked either to primary spaces around a courtyard or directly to the courtyard itself. Leo's reading of his apartment is cultivated by his years of living in a centrally organized dwelling rather than a linear one.

A series of simple diagrams, shown in figure 95, illustrates this role of the position of services for choice. At the top, the services are used to divide activities, typically between the household and member activities of a household. In the division, the house is linearly organized—one must move from one part through another to access the third. In the middle diagram, the services are organized around a central space (marked with a dashed "x"), so that all rooms have equivalent access to the courtyard. In the last diagram, the services and spaces are organized to support dual readings, either linear or concentric. One can read the spaces as sequentially ordered or as organized around a central space. Suburban housing production has provided a housing stock that is predominantly linearly organized, but the challenge for accommodating choice is to provide dwellings that support multiple readings.

Considering the assembled potential of a setting makes possible the emergence of an approach to the development of fabrics that is neither typological nor prototypical. It proposes that a fabric for dwelling is an assemblage of formal elements that constructs a field with both permanence and capacity for choice and change.

personal choice

There is broad consensus that personal choice in housing is fundamental. Contemporary approaches to providing choice include prototypical model homes, flexible homes, and custom homes. Although all these strategies provide options, they assume initial selection and adaptation as the modes for accommodating differences and changes in lifestyles. An argument for dwelling forms that enable multiple uses and associations over time is still a necessary complement to all the other approaches.

While selecting a model home is a kind of choice, it is a consumer-based selection that reflects one's immediate projection of lifestyle. Each space of the typical model home has a functional designation; each activity identified as part of a way of living is fulfilled on a space-by-space basis. In this way, the form of the house is said to be efficient. But increasing choice—through the formal structuring of capacity of access, claim, assemblage, and dimensions—is hardly inefficient. A house designed with the capacity to accommodate choice still fulfills a given program but has the potential to extend, change, and hold alternative programs as well. Increasing capacity does not inherently increase the size of a dwelling. If one designs dwellings on a programmatic basis, adding capacity on a room-by-room basis does add area to each activity. But the design of capacity is not programmatic—it is formal and spatial. The case study comparisons presented in this chapter argue against random generosity in sizes but argue for an organization that embeds capacity as a structured set of relations. In the long run, capacity continuously embedded in housing is more efficient and more sustainable than functionally specific housing.

Flexible homes provide an overall framework for subsequent personal decisions to be made by the resident. An argument for flexibility, defined as an unimpeded set of spaces that are sized to accommodate many changing activities, is not an argument for choice. A flexible space allows for an ambiguous fit[14] between the house's form and its potential activities by minimizing design features. Too often, the design of flexible spaces removes character and intensity from the form of a house, leaving a neutral, empty shell. Although many activities may fit, none seems to fit well. Residents no longer make choices in concert with the environment. Choice requires more than flexibility—it requires that the form of a space be able to evoke different meanings, associations, and actions for residents over time and for different households.

A third way of tailoring choices in housing is through user participation and custom house design, in which the projected or actual users participate in the design process and make choices before construction is completed. Although participatory approaches support choice making during the design stage, the danger again exists in limiting subsequent and everyday choices if capacity is not embedded in the setting. In any participatory process, decisions about form still need to be made.

Although San Francisco's fabric is representative of nineteenth- and early-twentieth-century typological development and Clayton's setting represents the contemporary prototypical approach, this comparison is not an argument for typological design. Instead, it argues for the need to embed capacity in settings to absorb diversity, not specificity, in ways of living. There is nothing in contemporary residential development and design that precludes supporting dwelling as diverse and temporal—all we need to change is to also require capacity in the performance of our housing.

Although the formal attributes of housing are not deterministic, they are material in enabling choice in everyday living. The form of the fabric has the potential to convey and receive impressions, inspiring a dialogue between place and inhabitant that is rich with a range of interpretations over time. Although there is no single design formula, method, or pattern to achieve this dialogue, it begins with a disciplined way of seeing choice in form and of structuring choice that is experiential rather than programmatic.

It does not help to just study how people behave in the context of a presumably static physical environment. Nor is it rewarding to study physical forms as response to assumed human behavior or need.

N. JOHN HABRAKEN

Supports: An Alternative to Mass Housing
(London: Architectural Press, 1972 [1961 in Dutch])

| sharing in a setting

THE NEED TO DESIGN FOR THE COMMON POSSIBILITIES OF DWELLING HAS LONG BEEN RECOGNIZED, but the urgency of this need has been renewed in recent suburban critiques.[1] The volumetric structuring of our suburban settings insulates households from each other, from the streets, and sometimes from the piece of yard or garden that represents the captured portion of the suburban landscape. This sense of isolation has led to a resurgence of interest in the seeking and building of community.

Today, the term *community* is widely cast over a multitude of social relationships and their design. To achieve a sense of community, we have community planning, community development, community meetings; we question how to rebuild community and then remember to ask what constitutes a good community. Is it small or large, ethnically distinct or demographically diverse? Is a community gated, with private facilities and roads, or does a sense of community require increased public amenities?

For the design professions, it is helpful to broadly distinguish between cultural and topographic communities. The first is spatially diffused—a network of relationships based on shared practices, ideas, experiences, and desires—and independent of the setting. The second is founded in a place, a particular locale. Historically, a cultural community was also based in a place. The growth of spatially diffuse networks, including the telephone, road systems, and information technologies, supported the dispersal of the cultural community away from a particular setting. Not surprisingly, this spread paralleled the rise in production of volumetric settings. As these settings minimized our connection to topographic communities, our dependence upon cultural connections increased. As a result, we seek community by calling, driving, and networking at school, at work, at church, and at the health club. But cultural networks need not be accepted as substitutes for the place-specific relations of dwelling. The two types of communities are complementary, not mutually exclusive. Thus, re-examining the relations of adjacency and proximity in a setting reveals alternatives for neighboring.

A neighborhood is defined by what the individual participants *share*— an interaction, an identity, or an everyday way of living. We measure the place of a neighborhood through the propensity of a setting to support and promote this sharing. A fundamental task of residential design is to explicitly build this propensity into the architecture. Although it is rare to find a setting that totally excludes ways of sharing, the degree of sharing and the approach to its design have consequences for dwelling.

infrastructural sharing

Most settings support sharing through an *infrastructure* of services and spaces that residents use in common. In settings supported by infrastructural sharing, common spaces and facilities are designed, owned, and maintained for collective use. These can include streets, sidewalks, recreational centers, golf courses, commercial centers, and courtyards, as well as common entries, mailboxes, or parking for a group of residences. This kind of sharing engenders a sense of community through interaction—through the opportunities to meet neighbors while using the shared facilities.

A distinction can be made between public and private infrastructural sharing. A public infrastructure is organized and maintained for public use, although the cost may be privately or publicly funded. In general, the spaces and facilities are accessible to all. A private infrastructure also supports collective use but is limited to a group of individuals who pay for the infrastructure and its maintenance through initial association fees or renewing home owners' fees. To use the facilities requires permission from the association or from a resident. All settings support sharing through their infrastructure—minimally through an access road and lot subdivision, more typically through a network of roads, subdivisions, and utilities.

In Radburn, residents share two independent infrastructures (figure 96). One is a public, vehicular network that provides access between the cul-de-sacs and the larger region and connects the houses to public facilities such as the commercial center, recreational facilities, and the school. Embedded in the road networks and cul-de-sacs are the sanitary sewers, storm drains, and water and gas lines. The other infrastructure is the network of pedestrian paths claimed by Radburn residents and maintained by the home owners' association, which provides access from homes to the Radburn parks and recreational facilities as well as the public school and commercial center. Although the houses are small and although the

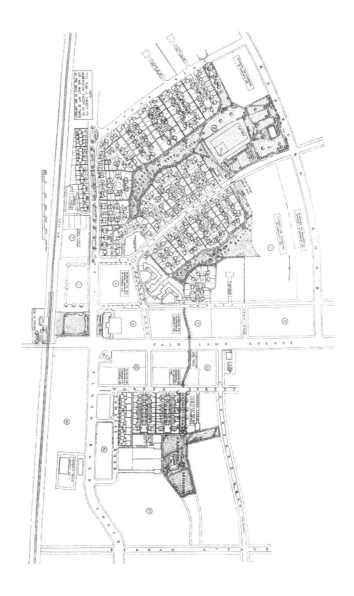

96. "Plan of Development at Radburn Completed by 1930," by Clarence S. Stein.

ways to enlarge them are strictly limited, residents choose to stay in Radburn because of its sense of community.[2] Not surprisingly, one remembers Radburn for its infrastructure, not its houses.

typological sharing

When emphasizing sharing through *type*, a setting is characterized by a repetitive assemblage of patterns—of forms, of spatial sequences, of materials, or of construction. Types support sharing through a collective recognition of these patterns and understanding of their use. Historically, this kind of residential sharing was developed on a unit-by-unit basis in which each dwelling was built as a variation and individual interpretation of an implicitly held sense of the local type.[3] A topographic community evolves

97. Cambridgeport.

98. Common Cambridgeport house types. *Left to right:* side hall plan, double plan, and quartered plan.

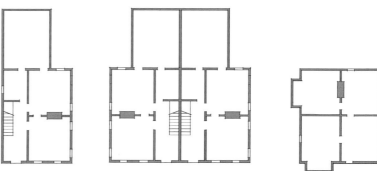

from the typological characteristics of dwelling—a physical identity as well as a collective understanding of how to live in a place.

Like other late-nineteenth- and early-twentieth-century American settings, Cambridgeport, in Cambridge, Massachusetts (figure 97), was developed typologically. At the infrastructural level, streets were gridded and the land was subdivided into rectangular lots that were deeper than they were wide, a pattern common for land speculators of the time. The houses were variations on several house types—a side hall house type was most common in the case study documented in this chapter (figure 98). Although there was no master plan or common facility for Cambridgeport when it was originally subdivided,[4] an incredibly rich character of dwelling emerged—simultaneously cohesive in community identity and individually varied (figure 99).

A Cambridgeport side hall house is composed of two rooms that open off the same side of an entry and access hall. If the house has two stories, the access hall contains a stair, and the second-floor plan repeats the first-floor plan. In houses of this type, the gable ends extend from the street to the rear yard. The first floor is elevated several feet above ground level, both for privacy and to accommodate any changes in grade.

chapter six

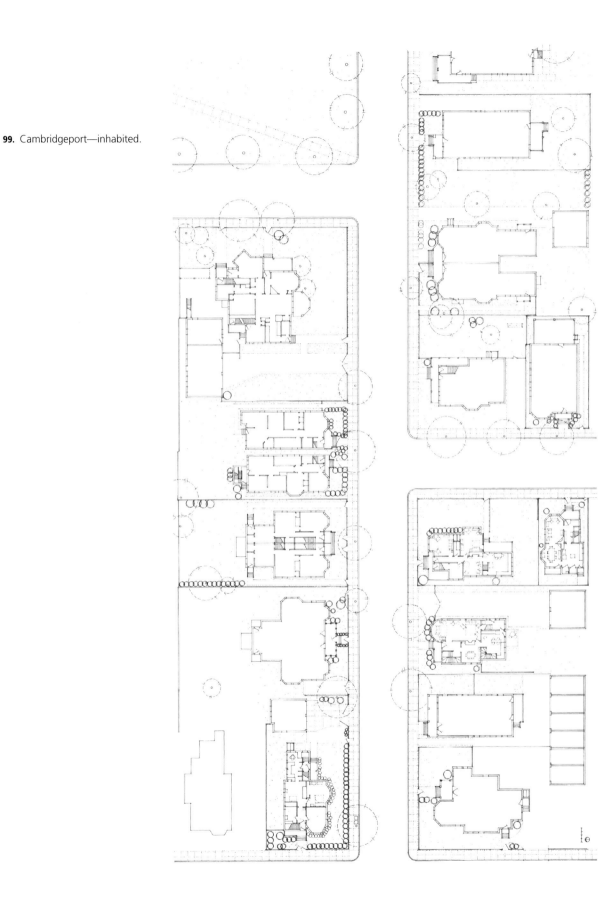

99. Cambridgeport—inhabited.

In the inhabited plan, the individual interpretations of the type are evident in the differences between the houses. One or both of the two rooms might have a bay window. The side hall is mirrored, and the outer wall of the side hall becomes a shared interior wall for the double plan. A front stoop or porch is either shared or divided between two households. In a two-family house, the households are divided in section rather than plan, with one household above the other. In this variation, the entry and access hall are configured in a variety of ways to provide entry to both units either from the porch or from an inner entry vestibule, and the stair is part of either the upper unit's space or the entry. The greatest variations on the type are at the rear of the houses, where one to two rooms are added, typically to hold a kitchen and eating area.

In this neighborhood, the use of a side hall house type engenders a sense of community in at least two ways. First, there is a sharing of physical identity, a recognizable collective appearance of the neighborhood. Second, because neighbors read and occupy spaces that are similar in their structure, they develop a common understanding about ways of living in the neighborhood.

What distinguishes Cambridgeport from residential settings built from prototypes and model homes is the rich variation between houses as well as the variety of individual interpretations in the use of the houses' spaces. The physical variation emerges from the use of type, the inhabitational variation from the use of a type embedded with capacity for choice.

The speculative land developers and builders of Boston's Back Bay, San Francisco's Victorians, or Charleston's single houses produced distinctly recognizable places, built of standardized elements and according to a type, yet each house is subtly different and capable of much adaptation. Efforts to extend this approach are difficult in today's building culture. First, the scale of development has grown. In the late nineteenth and early twentieth centuries, landowners subdivided large plots of land that were then sold to small-scale developers, builders, and individual home owners. A residential setting was assembled on a house-by-house basis, dependent upon a culture of like-minded but independent craftsmen and home owners who implicitly understood the use of a type. Today, developers not only subdivide and service land but also provide the houses and the collective facilities. Large areas are developed by a single entity. When quantity is a key factor in profitability, the demands of large-scale production typically override any single entity's ability to produce an effective range of variety. Second, having accepted the volumetric premises of dwelling, we no longer have a culture that *implicitly* accepts "constraints" on individual, privately owned buildings. Instead, we reject any interior constraints on space that would be suggested by a type. Efforts to reproduce the versatility of the nineteenth-century settings rely on explicit agreements to collaborate, such as design guidelines, regulations, and design reviews that are controlled and administered by central bureaucracies, agencies, and home owner associations that govern only the exteriors of houses.

territorial sharing

Are type and infrastructure sufficient to build a fabric? By themselves, they do not promote sharing as a connection of residents to their setting. Sharing requires something more—a territory that links dwelling with its setting. When this territory becomes a place that each resident inhabits, the presence of individuals and their differences are shared.

The Sachs Apartments illustrate such sharing. As described in the fourth chapter, all the residences are oriented toward the light and view of the valley. Bearing walls extend perpendicular from the hill, reinforcing this orientation. Household activities are layered in this structure—some occur in the darker, cavelike places against the hill, some in the diffuse light of the midzone. Each living unit is structured in this way. For example, in one unit, on the ground floor of the complex on the upper half of the hill, Schindler introduced overhead lights that are 2 feet wide (figure 100). These lights build zones of capacity that predominantly parallel the retaining walls and occasionally extend perpendicular from the hill. At the outer edge, the light zone no longer follows the perimeter of the unit but is set back 4 feet from the window edge. This 4-foot zone is key—the layer is thin, limiting the choices of activities to personal ones such as eating and

100. The Sachs Apartments—a dwelling unit with narrow bands of capacity throughout the unit and a wider, 4-foot zone along the window edge.

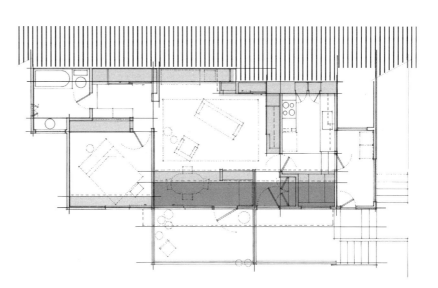

101a, b, c. The Sachs Apartments—personal choices at the edges of a dwelling unit.

102. The Sachs Apartments—dimensioned at one level.

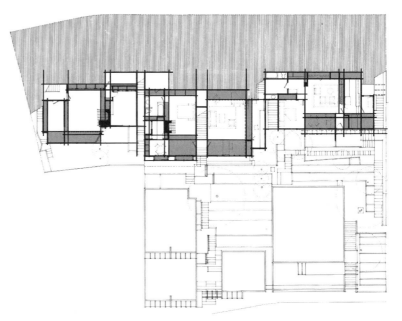

working (figures 101a–c) and allowing natural light to penetrate deeply into the unit and the activities within.

This is not a house-by-house pattern but an organization that extends across the setting from unit to unit (figure 102). The 4-foot zone is structured by walls, overhead light troughs, dropped ceilings, and balconies and is occupied differently across the setting—some households use the zone for writing, some for dining, some for sitting (figures 103a–d). It is a zone that extends the dimensional capacity of the primary spaces. The specific activity at the edge is selected by and unique for each household. As residents

chapter six

103a, b, c, d. The Sachs Apartments—territorial sharing across the individual units.

occupy these territories, they overlook the community paths and garden. Thus, sharing evolves individually through the habitation of a territory that connects a household with its neighbors.

This way of sharing is familiar, found in bay windows, porches, and stoops (figure 104).[5] Increasingly, when its door is open, the garage has become the new porch of the suburbs, a place where neighbors meet while tinkering on the car or at workbenches. In territorial sharing, it is the habitation—the particular ways in which people live—that builds a sense of community.

sharing in a setting

sharing as a fabric

The approaches to designing for sharing have consequences for promoting continuous qualities of a fabric or for reinforcing the volumetric characteristics of a setting. All settings, whether continuous or discrete, hold some infrastructure in common. The volumetric building of suburban communities depends predominantly upon infrastructural sharing. Given the intentionally independent relationship among the houses, residents leave their homes and move into the collective or public domain to interact with their neighbors and community. There is a cost associated with this way of sharing, whether it is supported by public taxes or private home owner fees. Infrastructural sharing requires a centralized organization with initial and long-term costs that each person pays, regardless of the degree to which he or she participates. When scale or cost prohibits development of extensive common structures, infrastructural sharing is minimized and potential for interaction is decreased. All too commonly, residents share only a road and land subdivision, a very uniform and car-dependent setting (figure 105).

The use of type produces a spectrum of detached dwelling environments, from volumetric to woven. When a type primarily organizes the house interior, the resulting setting has residual spaces between houses, characteristic of the volumetric setting. So, although the type organizes continuities across a setting through repetition, the outdoor space can be, and often is, omitted from the structure. In the previous Cambridgeport example, this discontinuity is evident in the outdoor spaces between houses (figure 106a). When a type incorporates the site—interior and exterior spatial relations as well as relationships to adjacent houses—a fabric emerges from the repetition of the type. Thus, in typological settings

105. Volumetric settings that depend upon the road for sharing: "Williamsburg Neighborhood," Nebraska; photograph by Ted Kirk.

106a, b. The spaces between houses—residual, as in Cambridgeport *(left)*, or integral, as in Charleston *(right)*.

107. Sharing in the setting—the Sachs Apartments.

such as San Francisco or Charleston (figure 106b), as well as prototypical settings such as Horatio West, indoor and outdoor spaces are integrated and integral to sharing.

Although territorial sharing can be embedded in a setting on a house-by-house basis, the place of a neighborhood is supported when the propensity to share is structured across several sites. Thus, the entries and bay windows of Cambridgeport and San Francisco collectively describe a zone across the façades of the houses. In the Sachs Apartments, a similar zone is structured across the downslope façades, but the forms of sharing vary from unit to unit—an outdoor balcony or patio as well as indoor bay windows, alcoves, or articulated edges (figure 107).[6] In the Sachs Apartments, a strong collective identity emerges even though the buildings were erected at different times, with differing floor plans.[7]

Both repetitive typological and systemic territorial approaches result in a shared structuring of a setting in form and for use. The lesson of the Sachs Apartments for detached dwelling is that when sharing is systemic, only the positions need to be held in common. This is critical in settings where only minimal infrastructure can be afforded or where less legislation of collective identity is desired. When detached dwelling is seen as a fabric, the task of collective design is redefined. The task is not to separate public from private or individual from community but to design a setting for one that is also the setting for sharing.

The word "dwelling" here means something more than having a roof over our head and a certain number of square meters at our disposal. First, it means to meet others for exchange of products, ideas and feelings, that is, to experience life as a multitude of possibilities. Second, it means to come to an agreement with others, that is, to accept a set of common values. Finally, it means to be oneself, in the sense of having a small chosen world of our own.

CHRISTIAN NORBERG-SCHULZ
The Concept of Dwelling: On the Way to Figurative Architecture
(New York: Electa/Rizzoli, 1985)

chapter seven | unpacking

the building of communities, the promise of autonomy and privacy that underlies the demand for detached houses should not be forgotten. In the suburbs, our home is our turf and our sanctuary.

In the volumetric suburb, our house is a castle, and our moat is a sea of neatly trimmed grass. Within our walls, we live as we please; outside our walls, we recognize our responsibilities as social beings. This simple dichotomy, fundamental to the structure of the volumetric setting, is sustained when the concepts of autonomy and privacy are coupled as equivalent. Underlying a shell-like structuring is the belief that to achieve autonomy or the freedom to choose, one needs privacy or the ability to control a defined area of space. This premise assumes that privacy removes constraints and limitations on one's behavior, with the corollary that greater privacy affords more choice.[1] To control visual, acoustic, and social access, a boundary needs to be defined that contains one's territory. The bounding element is the separating wall—and its permutations such as curtains, fences, and hedgerows—which is structured to define a perimeter of privacy. Since the volumetric suburb achieves both privacy and autonomy in such a direct and obvious manner, we not only accept boundaries but also reinforce their bounding characteristics.

the bounding wall

Acceptance of the bounding wall is all-pervasive in housing design, production, and marketing—a practice that reinforces and aggravates the problems of volumetric settings. The persistence of the box, as described in chapter 2, is coupled with the increasing dependence upon continuous walls, especially exterior walls, as the defining architectural elements of a house. Technical systems and innovations disappear within the walls, and the walls are then finished to a style, like gift boxes in wrapping paper, to make each house unique and expressive of its owner.

No other consumer product has changed so little in its appearance and functional performance over the past half century as the single detached house. Advances in technology and production have tended to be substitutional, supporting incremental, evolutionary changes in house form and the nature of the wall. Because the changes have been gradual, we fail to recognize how technical advances intensify the bounding character of the perimeter wall.

The walls of American suburbs are built of wood. Modern stud framing originated sometime in the mid- to late 1800s, brought about through the combination of two technological advances: the mass production of inexpensive nails and sawn lumber. The "balloon" stud frame replaced heavy timber framing, which was in turn replaced by platform-frame construction.

Balloon-framed wall studs were typically 4 × 4 inches and two to three stories in height. These studs were erected every 4 feet, sheathed with planks that readily spanned the 4-foot span between studs. By the early twentieth century, lumber sizes had decreased in both girth and length. The shorter, smaller 2 × 4–inch stud that replaced the 4 × 4 needed to be spaced from 16 to 24 inches on center. As moisture and shrinkage in wood were better controlled, "2 × 4" became nominal nomenclature for a 1.5 × 3.5–inch stud that needed to be spaced 16 inches on center. The shift from heavy timber to studs is significant to the quality of the exterior wall—timber framing is an open, linear framework of structural posts, beams, and lateral bracing with an independent system of closure. The repetitive stud wall system with sheathing works as a massive system that simultaneously serves as both structure and closure. As the stud diminished in size, the framing system became more dense and closed, with studs evenly distributed throughout any wall and spacing between studs less habitable by the human dimension.

In the 1960s, sheathing and cladding changed substantially. Sheet materials replaced board sheathing and subfloor diaphragms almost entirely: plywood or fiberboard began to be used on walls and plywood on subfloors and roofs. Gypsum board replaced lath and plaster interior finishes. As a consequence, greater lengths of solid walls are now easier to erect.

Heating, ventilating, and air conditioning equipment is smaller and centralized, designed so that the distribution systems can run through walls, eliminating radiators and floor and ceiling vents. The positions of walls tend to become more fixed, regardless of their structural role, as walls uniformly take on the role of servicing the house. Thermal comfort in a house presumes that every habitable interior space of a house should be uniformly controlled to a temperature set by the resident. Thermal and vapor barriers are placed in the exterior bounding wall of the house to maximize uniform thermal control. Thus, advances in thermal conditioning reinforce the solidity of exterior walls.

The history of thermal efficiency parallels the increase in functional efficiency of homes. When walls were cold and heat came from central, radiating sources, activities and furnishings were located away from the exterior walls and tended to float in the space of the rooms. Rooms were dimensioned and configured for a variety of activities to take advantage of the heat. Insulating the walls allowed activity spaces to grow smaller and more specialized, as furnishings and activities moved to occupy the perimeter of a room.

Resistance to fire is now calculated on the basis of the layers of sheathing on walls and roofs, and structurally efficiency is maximized when sheathing is positioned at the perimeter of the house. As in thermal control, efficient technical performances in fire and structural design also reinforce the solidity of the exterior wall.

The evolutionary creep toward a solid exterior wall intensifies the volumetric problems in the suburbs. If we continue to accept the premise that containing walls are a necessity for privacy, and that privacy is a prerequisite for autonomy, then suburbs cannot change and will continue to isolate households inside boxes. We need to question whether the most efficient technical solutions should direct housing design or whether a setting for dwelling should be premised on the possibilities of connections—between households and with the setting—to account more fully for all of our setting. Can the box be unpacked without forsaking privacy and autonomy?

beyond the picture window: assembling a field

Achieving continuity without visual connection is relatively straightforward. For example, there is continuity of dimensional relations, achieved by positioning elements to relate with each other through a common reference line or plane. In Levittown, as in many suburban settings, the fronts of all the houses are positioned at nearly equal distances from the street edge, along an implied line that builds a continuous, set-back street edge.

There is connection through continuity of access. As a system, access structures relations from the regional to the local and vice versa. We move between rooms within a house, into the yard, into the street, into the city, and into the landscape. Access can be described as continuous when its structure bridges relations between levels, when each part of the access extends a system throughout the setting. Comparison of Clayton and San

Francisco illustrates the difference between discontinuity and continuity of access (figures 108 and 109). In both settings, one moves into the yards or lots of each house by turning 90 degrees from the street. In San Francisco, access then shifts to planes above or below the street level but continues directly from the yard into the entry and through part of the house

108. Clayton—access overlay.

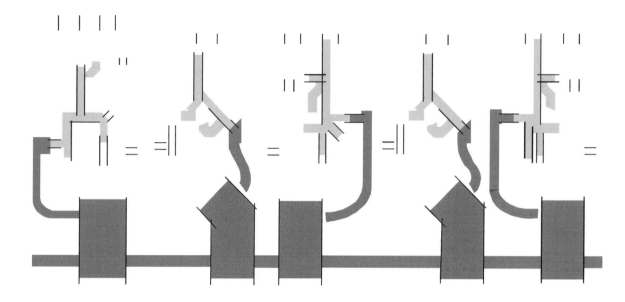

109. San Francisco—access overlay.

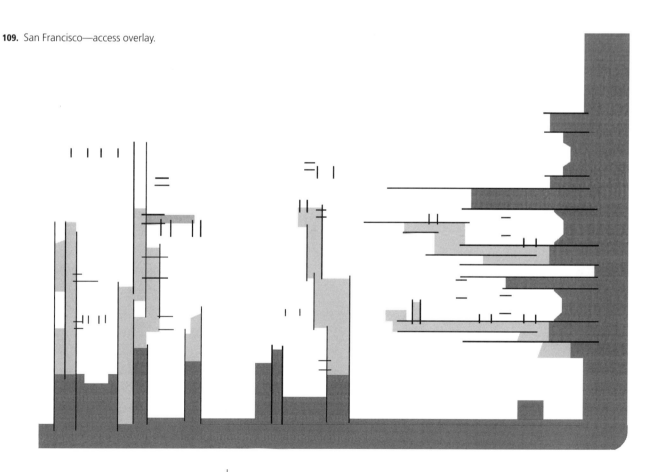

before the spatial configuration transforms. In Clayton, one moves onto the driveway in front of the garage, and a path links the drive to the front door of each house. In some cases, this link is quite direct; in others, the end of the path is the only clue to finding the front door. In Clayton, access within houses is organized independently of the exterior system, with patchwork links between the two. The experience of moving from street to house or from house to street is disjointed.[2]

Although continuities such as dimension and access can be achieved without challenging the walled character of the volumetric setting, the bounding walls still need to be questioned if the problems of separation and residual, wasted spaces are to be addressed. If houses are to be a fabric for dwelling, all areas of a setting need to be part of the structure; this requires formal competence in making visual and spatial connections as well as separations.

At first glance, the solutions already seem to be in place—the ubiquitous picture window and sliding glass door. In a typical 1950s house, the picture window faced the street, letting the visitor see a bit of the inside of the house and letting the resident see the street. The sliding glass door was in back, giving both view and access to a rear yard. Fifty years later, the picture window has disappeared as suburban houses turn their backs on the street, with large panes of glass relocated to the sides and rear façades of houses. Though touted as providing spaciousness and view, these icons of suburban living are no more than enlarged holes that maintain the plane of the wall in which they are located. As such, the picture window and sliding glass door do not form a physical sense of connection between two spaces but preserve a sense of separation and boundary. Although these larger forms of opening increase light and visibility, they nonetheless maintain the boundary of the house and the volumetric structure of the setting. Since privacy and autonomy in the volumetric setting are structured through the building enclosure, many households find themselves covering the "holes."

A more generalized approach to understanding connections as spatial continuities—including light and view—is more readily achieved when the concepts of privacy and walled containment are uncoupled. In housing, this requires discarding the assumption that complete containment and privacy must be coincident at the inside-outside perimeter of the house. Such uncoupling is already common: for example, it is quite typical for the back yard of a lot to be fenced. Thus, the perimeter or containment for privacy is at the lot line, independent of (and, in this case, larger than) the boundary of the house. At the edge between house and yard is the opportunity to build connection and indicate a transition rather than enclosure and separation. Although this particular uncoupling increases the connection between a household's interior and exterior spaces, it still

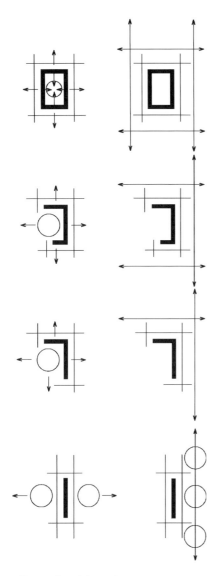

110. Forms of containment.

tends to isolate one household from the next, maintaining separation at the lot line rather than at the shell of the house.

To "indicate" transitional spaces requires seeing and designing with the spatial qualities of walls, not just their functional capabilities. Typically, walls are used to divide—the broad faces of the plane of the wall are used to separate activities of a program. Less commonly used in housing design is the directional nature of a wall. Activities positioned in parallel to the plane of a wall are read as connected. Although these concepts are not new to architecture, the dominance of dividing walls to delimit residential spaces needs to be challenged. Both planar phenomena need to be present to change suburban settings from volumes to fabrics. To make planar surfaces both divide and connect, their assemblage needs to be reconsidered—their spatial relationships to access, to each other, and to dimensions.

Examining the case studies again reveals alternatives for structuring spaces in suburban settings. Some settings embody the two characteristics of planar surfaces by positioning the walls in parallel, embedding a sense of transparency and connection along the planes as well as a sense of separation across the walls. Other settings both direct and contain by assembling walls through partial containments,[3] simply described as L, C, and U forms (figure 110).

In the Sachs Apartments, Rudolf Schindler used a parallel structuring of walls, connecting each household from the nearby gardens and courtyards to the distant view of the valley and opposing hillside.[4] Although the main spatial direction of each space is toward the larger landscape, the access within each unit moves across and perpendicular to the walls. The experience is one of moving through a layering of activities. First you enter the central bay or bays of an apartment. Upon entering, you are drawn to the light and into the space, in parallel with the walls. If you continue along the walls (read as connecting) and out toward the landscape, the kitchen and eating areas emerge behind the wall along which you entered. If you move directly ahead at the entry, you must move through a wall (read as privacy) to reach the bed and bath areas. After you move into the bed or kitchen area, the next wall is a barrier between the household and any activity on the other side. In this field of walls, the smallest dimensions between parallel walls are spaces between units. These spaces, though narrow and not part of any unit, are never residual but are part of the access between the top and the middle of the hill. Thus, by the position of entries and the direction of access, the parallel walls both connect and divide the spaces of the hillside for dwelling (figure 111).

A similar parallel structuring of walls and zones can be found in the San Francisco case study but with an important distinction: the interior and exterior access moves through the field of walls in parallel rather than

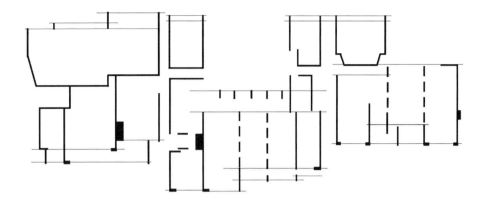

111. The Sachs Apartments—
walls in a directional field.

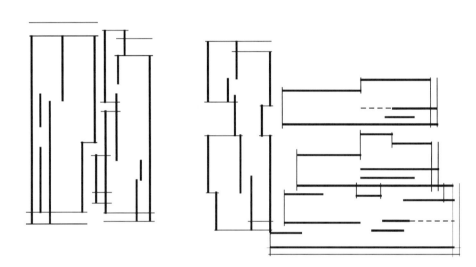

112. San Francisco—
walls in a directional field.

perpendicularly (figure 112). In a setting structured by narrow lots, the parallel direction of walls and access emphasizes connections along the length of the house, from the front to the rear. Privacy within the house and between neighbors is readily maintained, even with windows deeply embedded in the site, because of the clear directionality of the solid walls with openings in the perpendicular direction. Windows rarely look upon other neighbors' activities, indoor or out. Thus, connection and privacy are not mutually exclusive when the dual properties of the wall are encouraged within the overall structure of a site or setting.

Assembled planes in which some spatial boundaries are implied rather than delimited define partially contained spaces. Such an assembly of walls inherently defines an activity area, reminiscent of the completely contained form. Yet a partially contained space is also open and connects toward space beyond the implied demarcation. Like the parallel walls, contained spaces are directional, but the experience has a terminus in the defined space. Thus, the partially contained territory has a center focus

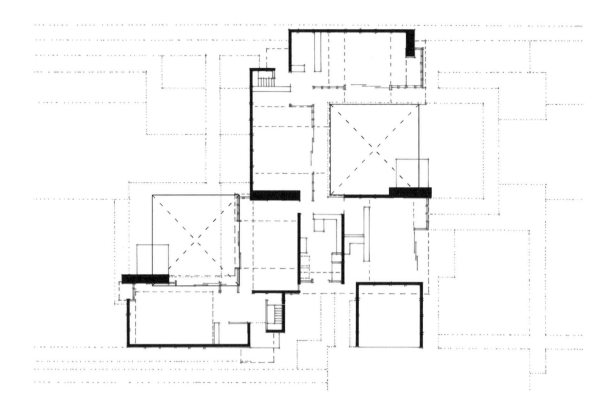

113. Kings Road—partially containing walls.

114. Pueblo Ribera.

similar to the completely contained space as well as an extension and connection to spaces beyond itself. Privacy in the setting is controlled through the position, direction, and relation of partially contained spaces with other elements and systems in the structure of the field.

In both the Kings Road House[5] and Pueblo Ribera Court,[6] Schindler used a C-shaped form of partial containment. In Schindler's personal residence on Kings Road (figure 113), five of these containments define the major activity spaces for two families. Four of the Cs are grouped in two pairs that form two Ls, which in turn partially contain two gardens. The walls are assembled from tilt up concrete panels, defining a space with a concrete "back" and garden "front." The outer edges of the walls serve not only as separators—barriers from the street or partitions from other spaces—but also as garden walls that extend the inner space of another C.

In Pueblo Ribera (figures 114 and 115), Schindler again used partial, C-shaped forms, this time pouring the walls in 16-inch increments within sliding concrete forms. Unlike the room-level assemblage of Cs that formed the two units in Kings Road, each C in Pueblo Ribera corresponds with one household.[7] A space within any C has the same back-to-front, inside-to-outside quality as Kings Road. The outer edges of the Cs

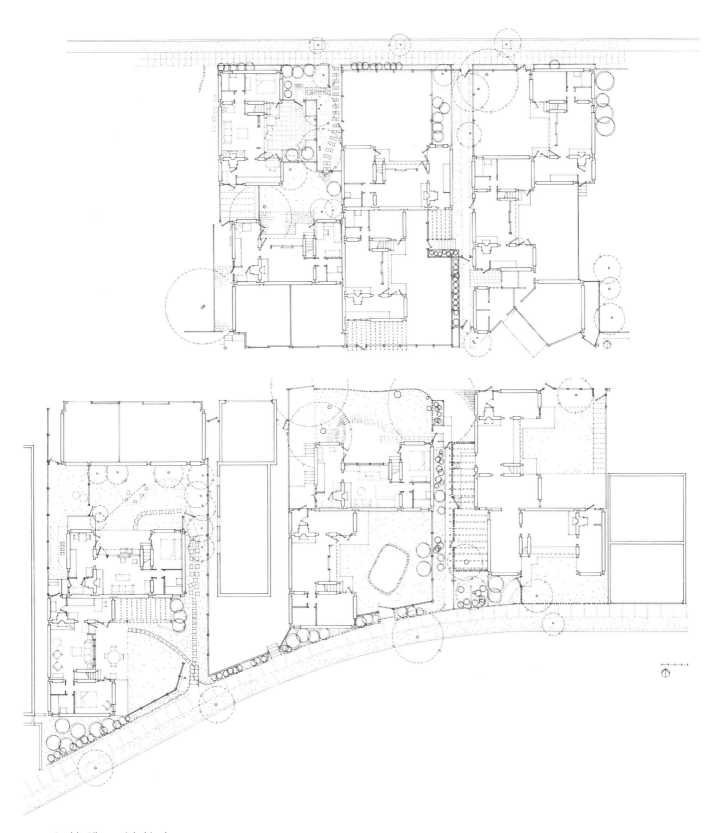

115. Pueblo Ribera—inhabited.

116. Pueblo Ribera—partially containing walls.

are the garden walls of another unit, accentuating inside-to-outside connections for a neighbor (figure 116).

Partial containment also structures the Charleston setting as a single detached dwelling fabric (figure 117). The long, rectangular houses of Charleston are organized perpendicular to the street and positioned with mostly solid masonry walls on the northern property line; the front façade is positioned adjacent to the sidewalk. A covered porch runs parallel along the length of the house. Within the house, the front room, entry/stair, and back room face the side yard. Centered on the north wall of each room is a fireplace flanked on both sides with bookcases, shelves, or alcoves. On the south wall are windows to the porch. The windows often extend to the ground, acting as doorways between the room and porch. The partial containment in the houses can be described as an E or L, again with a spatial orientation toward the gardens.

The Charleston setting is structured with detached Es or Ls, all oriented in the same direction, with the long wall to the north and the short wall parallel to the street.[8] As in the Schindler houses, walls serve both to

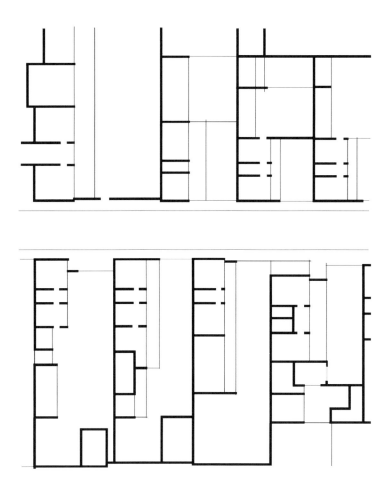

117. Charleston—partially containing walls.

118a, b. Charleston—connecting and separating.

connect and to separate. Inside the containment, the wall serves as barrier, separating household from street and neighbor while connecting to the side yard and, sometimes, to the rear. Outside, the short end of the containment—the house façade—builds the street edge. The north wall serves as a garden wall for a neighbor, and the length of the wall links the garden with the street. The importance of the previously described front doors of the Charleston house as a device to transform the setting becomes clearer within the description of the contained structure of the setting. When the door is closed, the containment of the street wall is extended, and the porch serves as transition between house and yard. When the door is open, the connection between the street and the garden is widened, and the porch serves as transition between house and street (figures 118a–b).

By now, the contribution of walled forms that describe complete containment to the generation of volumetric settings should be evident. But complete containment can also be woven as a fabric. In Irving Gill's Horatio West,[9] the entire complex of four houses and two apartments is assembled with a combination of partial and complete containments (figure 119). One room within each house is completely contained.

These contained rooms are positioned within the courtyard complex to structure relations: in serving as solid objects, they screen one house's activities from another, both along and across the central path. Displaced forward of the rest of the house, they redirect access from the path to the house. These rooms, on both the first and second floors, contain the greatest variety of resident uses, such as bedrooms to guest rooms, studies, and family rooms. Rather than being defined on a house-by-house basis, complete containment is discriminatingly deployed at scales either larger or smaller than a house.

A consequence of using fields of walls to weave a fabric is a loss of complete autonomy. In the above examples, a resident is no longer completely self-governing. Since households are dependent upon a neighbor's walls, residents are no longer free to do whatever they desire with the physical structure of the house. In the Charleston fabric, there is a loss of autonomy for each household over the north and street façades, since the partially containing walls structure the collective setting and relations between neighbors. Yet the loss of autonomy over two walls gives greater autonomy for use and change over the remainder of each household's house and lot. Given the density of our contemporary suburbs, few home owners have complete autonomy over their house and lot, as evidenced by the legal processes that have evolved to mediate battles between neighbors. The reality, unacknowledged by the volumetric production of housing, is that neighboring homes affect each other and the ways that households live. If we acknowledge that there is no autonomous suburban house, then the relations between houses can and should be structured in productive ways (figures 120a–c). Rather than separating all household activities from the setting, one can choose to be a part of or apart from a place.

119. Horatio West Court Apartments—experiential, built/unbuilt, and contained representations. While the built-unbuilt plan shows the perimeter of the inside-outside line of the house, it is not the same as the containment.

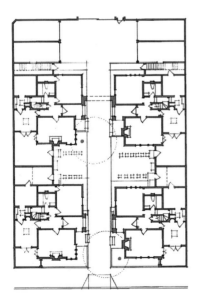
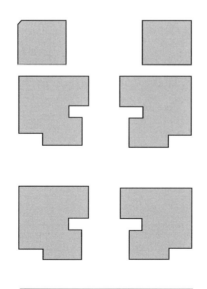
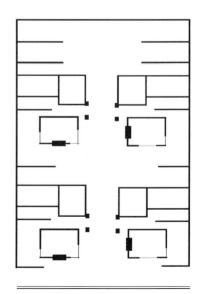

chapter seven

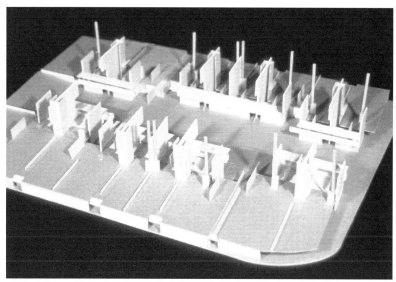

120a, b, c. Containment explored in a three-dimensional module.

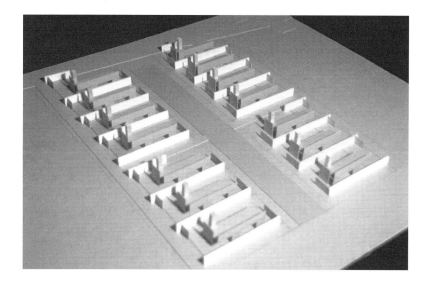

building connections

In the building of dwelling fabrics where walls no longer entirely delimit and bound a room or house, a competence in building forms of connection becomes a necessary complement to knowledge of the construction of walls. If the picture window is only a larger opening that maintains the plane of a wall, what other methods can be used to achieve connection?

One alternative can be seen at Pueblo Ribera and Kings Road in the definition of closure between the concrete walls. The open end of this "C" is protected by an overhanging eave, carried by two beams spanning the open end of the room and infilled with sliding doors. The shapes of the rooms, their orientation to the patios, and the displaced roof levels with resulting clerestory all contribute to a spatial interlocking (figures 121–122). Whether one is inside the house or in the garden, there are multiple ways to interpret what constitutes inside or out. The same can be seen in San Francisco, where shifting planes makes it possible to find reciprocal relations in both plan and section (figure 123). They suggest edges but do not contain.

121a, b. Pueblo Ribera—connecting edge.

122. Pueblo Ribera—inhabiting the edge. On the right, the building section as designed by Schindler. To the left, subsequent changes of the connecting edge made by the residents.

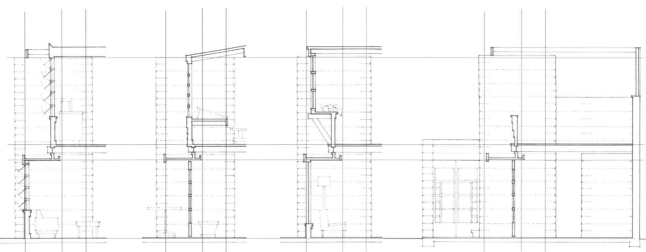

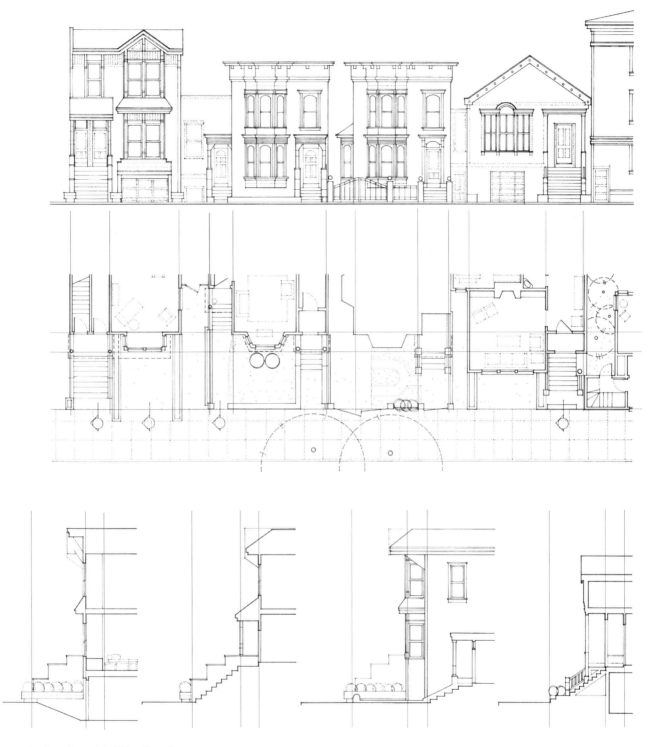

123. San Francisco—inhabiting the edge.

124a, b, c. Charleston—three readings of the porch.

Another form of connection is an articulated "third" space that serves as a transition layer between inside and outside. The porch is a familiar example of such a third space. The typical "front" porch runs parallel to and between the street and house façade, building a layer between public and private as well as indoor and outdoor. Residents and visitors alike interpret the porch as a territory associated with both the house and the street. In some neighborhoods, the porch is a shared space between neighbors and welcomes the public. In other cultures, a porch belongs to a household, with the household's claim extending to the transitional space—one enters the porch only if invited by the residents. The porch connects because it has the potential to be read as both inside and out (figures 124a–c).

As a form, the joint or third space can be deployed in a setting to seam houses to streets and yards, but the interior spaces adjoining the porch may be unaffected by the attachment, and dwelling may remain contained and separated. In many contemporary houses, the living areas now adjoin the back yard, with bedrooms displaced to the street side. For privacy reasons, these rooms tend to orient not to the street but to the side or rear yards. Nonetheless, the houses continue to have porches on the front façade in hopes of engendering a sharing between household and setting. Although the transition space continues to imply both inside and outside readings, the volumetric nature of the setting is unchanged. The interior and exterior are not linked. To connect, not just join, a transition needs to be layered within a spatial structuring of a setting.

At the Sachs Apartments, a layered transition zone also spans between the directional walls (figure 125). On the uphill façade, Schindler employs another form of connection, an assembly of small walls that are turned

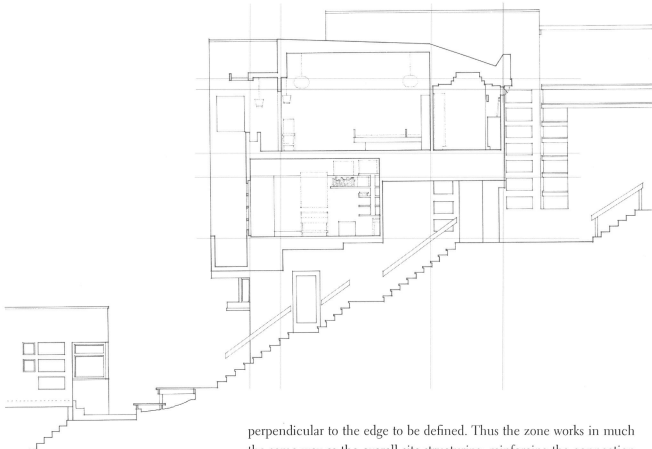

125. The Sachs Apartments—downhill and uphill connecting edges.

perpendicular to the edge to be defined. Thus the zone works in much the same way as the overall site structuring, reinforcing the connection between two sides of an implied zone. As these walls are, in turn, infilled to delimit the interior from exterior, the zone and direction are emphasized over the bounding (figures 126–127).

To structure connections within a fabric, some fundamental assumptions and practices about efficiencies need to be reconsidered. For instance, do all spaces of a house need to be uniformly tempered? If we are willing to enjoy a range of comfort levels throughout a house, the barrier between inside and outside can become more layered. The question for design then becomes: What kind of thermal control is required, and where is it located? The control becomes uncoupled from the exterior perimeter, and conditioning can be layered in a setting.

The same can be asked of "efficient" lateral bracing and uniform cavities in all walls for services. Even though the lateral bracing for a house is most efficiently achieved by erecting plywood panels at the perimeter of the house, should shear be the defining criterion for dwelling form? Do the wiring and plumbing need to be able to run everywhere in a house? If the answer is no to any of these questions, then opportunities arise that take advantage of the inherent tectonic characteristics in the assembling of systems to build connections in the setting while maintaining household privacy and autonomy.

126a, b. *Top:* The Sachs Apartments—façades facing the hill.

127. *Bottom:* Shifting planes to both enclose and connect—diagrams of transition layers assembled by adding, subtracting, displacing, and turning walls at an edge.

In the suburbs, a sense of connection to a setting, both the social and the natural, is not achieved by replacing more walls with glass. This sense of being both part of and apart from a place comes not just from redefining the edges and borders of houses but from deep within the structure of a setting, from a considered organization of containment that structures privacy and autonomy without forsaking the possibilities of moving beyond the wall.

Implicit in all Aldo van Eyck's writings and building is the notion that the minimalist Modern plan, the box, is functionally and psychologically inadequate. Transitions between inside and out, for instance, need articulating by thresholds and bays so as to emphasize the experience of negotiating them.

PETER BUCHANAN, LIANE LEFAIVRE, AND ALEXANDER TZONIS
Aldo and Hannie van Eyck: Recent Work: Two = Twee
(Amsterdam: Stichting de Beurs van Berlage, 1989)

chapter eight | designing density

MUCH OF U.S. SETTLEMENT CAN BE CHARACTERIZED AS LOW DENSITY—ONE- OR TWO-STORY BUILDINGS equally distributed on privately owned lots. This low-density pattern has proliferated, fueled by a view of the country as a land of open horizons with landscape to spare, a belief in technologies, a reliance upon mass production, an abundance of wood, and economic policies that favor decentralized home ownership.

Shifts in approaches to housing delivery changed the quality of dwelling from a sense of being *in* a place to one of building *on* a site. As the land developer took on the additional role of housing provider, the practice of house building was combined with the development of infrastructure and parceling of land. With the onset of a more centralized, larger-scale conveyance of houses, production efficiency guided design. Mass-produced, consumer-oriented approaches to house building and sales flourished, transforming the model home from ideal and example into prototype—a mass-produced standard with options. As a result, the design of dwelling became divorced from the particulars of place, and the low-density patterns that emerged after World War II became increasingly volumetric, with sharp distinctions between internal and external patterns that emphasized the shell of a house as divider. These prototypical houses, each centered on a lot, quickly drew ridicule and were criticized for being socially isolating and physically homogeneous. Yet, despite the criticism, the financial, social, and cultural allure of the single-family detached house increased, and the low-density pattern spread.

In the last two decades, scrutiny of the suburbs has revived. The horizon no longer seems endless. In our older suburbs, the limits are real. Towns are completely bordered by neighboring communities; there is no room to expand. These real limits are revitalizing the use of the existing housing stock and undeveloped pockets of land. At the suburban edge, limits to growth are being debated and imposed. With recognition of the long-term costs and losses of sprawl, the urban limit line—perhaps better called a suburban limit line—has emerged, beyond which the regional infrastructure can or should no longer support development. Both these real and imposed limits transform our impressions of endless, inexpensive land into concerns about scarcity, which in turn change our assumptions about land use and cost. The toll on our environment, the decay of older communities, and changing demographics amplify the cry to increase density—for cost, for sustainability, for community. This call is answered in a variety of ways, from the reconfiguration of lots to the reintroduction of walkable suburban centers.

Narrow lots, shallow lots, nonrectangular lots—the reordering of the subdivision at the lot level is now the normative way to achieve greater density. The amount of outdoor space is designed to a programmatic minimum, with side yards relegated to serving only as buffer zones. The lots themselves are reconfigured—z-lots, zipper-locks, and more amorphous shapes are proposed that build more houses on smaller lots.[1] But the underlying conception of house as box goes unchallenged, and suburban settings continue to be volumetric. Density is increased by packing and stacking volumes in ever-tighter configurations. In one California suburb, the local paper describes the resulting situation: "Concord's density sweepstakes start with 65 two-story houses planned on 7.5 acres. Each house would sit on lots of from 0.05 to 0.07 acres (14–20 units per acre), so small and cramped that backyard spas may have to be lowered in with cranes."[2] In these kinds of configurations, the outdoor backyards are like fishbowls, under the scrutiny of surrounding neighbors. Spaces between houses are narrower and used even less by residents, resulting in a finer, denser grain of wasted outdoor space (figure 128).

128. Pittsburg, California: an example of increasing density by packing houses closer together. Photo by Karl Mondon.

"New Urbanist" approaches, including neotraditional developments and transit-oriented developments, have raised our collective consciousness about the state of our suburbs. At the core of these approaches is a dense, pedestrian-oriented plan that appropriates urban qualities of both continuity and density through street planning, mixed-use development, and attached building types. Intensive networks and zoning regulations guide development of housing toward a collective structure for the community. Outside these centers, New Urbanist approaches depend mostly upon infrastructural ways of sharing to collectively organize what continues to be volumetric housing. As a result, outside the suburban nodes, the volumetric model is unaffected by these strategies, with increases in density still achieved by strategic positioning of housing masses on lots.

Suburban dwellers suffer losses of autonomy and privacy as their houses are positioned closer together, and relations between neighbors are increasingly litigious. In our more tightly packed suburbs, the regulations that govern relations between neighbors are increasing, as evidenced by the proliferation of home owner associations, city design reviews, elaborate zoning appeals, and long lists of criteria that constitute design guidelines. These processes are symptomatic of the volatility of the disputes that can erupt between neighbors whenever building changes are proposed.

It's time we acknowledge that the independent house does not exist. There can be no change in a setting that does not affect an adjacent household's sense of the neighborhood. Rather than regulate relations, we need to structure the density of our relations, acknowledging that dwelling is inherently connected and that change is inevitably part of a setting.

defining density

How does a view of suburban space as fabric transform assumptions about achieving greater density? To assess the possibilities, we must understand commonly held assumptions about the definition of *density*. Density typically is described as a ratio, a comparison either of use per unit of land or of built area per unit of land area, as illustrated in figure 129.[3] The former includes dwelling units and people per acre; the latter includes floor area ratios as well as open space coverage. Although both kinds of ratios quantify an environment, they fail to describe the physical structure of density. Without such a description, numerically defined objectives favor volumetric approaches to increasing density.

In volumetric settings, greater numerical density is achieved by packing more program in more units on more lots. If we compare Levittown in the 1950s and Clayton in the 1990s to examine this trend, Clayton's numbers indicate greater density than Levittown in every kind of measurement. In

case study	area measures			density measures				
	avg. lot size	square feet/ building	square feet/ dwelling unit	lots/acre	dwelling unit/ acre	residents/ acre	floor area ratio	open space ratio
Cambridgeport 1992	5,507	2,760 (1,000–5,800)	1,380	7.1	14.2	43	0.5	0.75
Charleston–North 1888 2000	5,140 5,140	4,631 4,424	4,631 4,424	7.9 7.9	7.9 7.9	31	0.9 0.86	0.62 0.62
Charleston–South 1888 2000	4,084 4,084	2,399 2,387	2,399 1,671	9.1 9.1	9.1 11.4	24–40	0.51 0.51	0.74 0.74
Clayton 1997	5,085	2,665 (2,100–3,060)	2,665	7.5	7.5	30	0.52	0.61
Horatio West 1980	2,156/8,625	1,890	1,890	4.4	17.6	40	0.88	0.52
Levittown Original 1998	6,000	750 1,050 (750–1,800)	1,050	6.8 (6.3–7.3) 6.8 (6.3–7.3)	6.8 (6.3–7.3) 6.8 (6.3–7.3)	15–25 15–25	0.13 0.18 (0.13–0.3)	0.87 0.82
Pueblo Ribera 1923 1980	4,507 4,507	648 840 (648–1,584)	648 916	8.34 8.34	16.7 15.3	25	0.35 0.43	0.65 0.65
Quadruple Housing 1903	5,904	3,900	3,900	6.2	6.2	31	0.66	0.64
Radburn Original 1992	4,563	1,503 (1,320–1,520) 1,975 (1,460–2,400)	1,503 1,975	9.1 9.1	9.1 9.1	27 27	0.33 0.43	0.82 0.78
Sachs Apts. 1980	2,944	2,457 (1,100–4,100)	965	11.7	42.1	50	1.16	0.43
San Francisco 1997	2,500	3,234	1,437	15	35	60	1.31	0.42
Notes	net	incl. garage	incl. garage	gross	gross	gross	net	net

129. Comparing densities as quantities.

Levittown, the average lot size is 60 by 100 feet, or 6,000 square feet; in Clayton, the lot is substantially narrower, 45 feet wide, and slightly longer at 113 feet, with a total area of 5,085 square feet—more than 900 square feet smaller. Therefore, in Clayton, there are more houses on smaller lots, and the number of residents accommodated almost doubles that of the original Levittown setting. This is achieved largely by a more than threefold increase in the size of each house. The decrease in open space ratio from

Levittown to Clayton reflects the larger house on a smaller lot. By all accounts, Clayton is denser than Levittown.

Despite the increase in the amount of building and numbers of residents, the physical structures of these two settings are remarkably similar: houses organized within a shell, centered on lots guided by setbacks, with paths of access linking street to front door. This increase in density has been achieved without reconfiguring the structure of the setting. Even though there are more buildings and more residents in Clayton, the overall effect is a more intensely homogeneous setting. The packing of housing volumes in ever-tighter adjacency provides more housing but amplifies the criticism directed toward the suburbs. It is in these denser suburban settings that the argument for the design of detached houses as a fabric becomes most compelling.

designing a fabric

The design of a fabric requires that characteristics of dwelling be seen as systemic—that attributes extend continuously throughout a setting. As such, a view of dwelling as a fabric provides structural definitions of density that complement numerical definitions. This view allows designers to see not just how many people can live in a setting but alternatives for how more people can live together. In addressing the question of how to achieve more dwelling, the objectives for the design of a fabric become more focused—with greater collective and individual choice, increased spatial possibilities, and decreased interstitial waste.

To achieve these objectives, the analyses of the case studies suggest a variety of propositions for settings as fabrics. First, the attributes of dwelling need to be systemic across its lot, its immediate locale. Rather than independent orders for house and site, the attributes of dwelling should be structured between inside and outside, from space to space, and in ways that account for the entire site—within and beyond the limits of any house. A capacity for greater individual and household choice should be embedded in the site.

Second, the attributes of any site should be systemic with its setting, extending, transforming, and participating in the larger constructed and topographic landscape. A fabric should organize relations among houses and sites as collective and should organize individual actions as collaborative. As density increases, detached houses are inevitably codependent and require clearer structures that hold the capacity for more complex collective choices.

Third, dwelling needs both permeability and separation. As the density of volumetric houses increases, associations with a setting seem to be at odds with desires for privacy: the walls that surround and protect our privacy from prying eyes also exclude us from views and connections to our gardens, neighbors, and the landscape beyond. Yet detached houses can be linked when a fabric is assembled with forms of both connection and separation. Giving a fabric permeability—a structure for connecting spaces—as well as containment makes it possible to account for all elements of a site, both indoors and outside. The interstitial pockets of wasted land can and should be eliminated from a setting by giving equal consideration to the spatial relations between the built and unbuilt.

A fourth proposition for dwelling calls for embedding depth in a setting. In any setting, every space has the potential to be interpreted as more than a single area. For example, within a plot of land, there are areas associated with the street and with adjoining neighbors. Within a house, alcoves or fireplaces define territories within rooms. In a fabric, these territories should be structured throughout the setting. The number of areas that can be perceived while passing through a site gauges the depth of a setting.[4] By providing a greater number of public-to-private thresholds, one can increase the potential to extend public access into the depth of a site. This in turn increases the capacity of the "back" of a site to hold additional building or units.[5]

By implication, then, some settings can be characterized as shallower and others as deeper to public access. In a shallow setting, a separating wall or boundary is built at or very near the street lot line. The entry gate and wall demarcate a clear boundary—an uninvited visitor is not welcome to move farther into the depth of the site. In the urban context, single-family townhouses and courtyard houses are often shallow to public access. In the suburban context, where houses are often set back from the street, the erection of fences around the front yard decreases the depth to public access (figure 130).

In most suburban settings, the perceived public depth is shallow, typically the depth of the front yard. There are two thresholds in this depth: one at the sidewalk—or at the street if there is no sidewalk—and one at the front door. There are two common routes through this depth: one from the sidewalk onto the drive and from the drive to the front door; the other from the sidewalk through the yard to the front door. In today's suburbs, both dense and dispersed, this depth and these routes dominate any particular setting, regardless of the degree of variation in the façades of the houses and model homes. There is an inevitable sameness in that depth (figure 131).

130. *Top:* No depth—walled fence at sidewalk.

131. *Bottom:* Shallow depth—front yard.

chapter eight

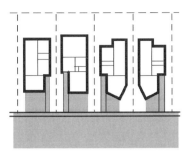

132. *Left:* Clayton: diagram showing thresholds at the sidewalk, the garage, and then the front door.

133. *Right:* More depth in Clayton.

In Clayton and Levittown, the depth is one zone deeper. Although the general structure of links from sidewalk to drive to front door is similar to that of the examples above, in Clayton, the front doors are positioned deeper in their sites. The thresholds then are read at the sidewalk, the garage door, and the front door. This additional zone in the setting holds the garage and services of the house—a buffer between household and street. Therefore, the entry must be deeper in the setting to bring a visitor around the garage (figures 132 and 133).

Levittown is either one or two zones deep. As discussed in an earlier chapter, the initial position of the house on a Levittown lot was off center, leaving room for a car to be parked by the side of the house. The service door to the kitchen opened to this side yard space. Although the first two thresholds are again at the sidewalk and front door of the house, there is an additional area or territory defined at the side of the house that can be read as publicly accessible. If the entry to the house is reached by moving into the drive first, then the depth can be read. The perceived depth is much shallower if one moves from the sidewalk directly on a path to the front door (figures 134 and 135).

134. *Left:* Levittown: diagram showing two routes with different depths, the deeper one at the drive and the shallower one at the walk.

135. *Right:* More depth in Levittown.

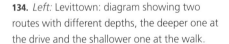

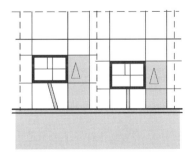

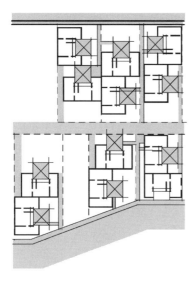

136. *Left:* Pueblo Ribera: diagram showing pedestrian access moving into the depth of each lot, both from the street and from the alley.

137. *Right:* More depth in Pueblo Ribera.

From these shallower to deeper examples, a pattern emerges suggesting that to perceive depth in a setting requires structuring access in a setting rather than linking node to node. For example, Pueblo Ribera Courts doubles the number of units per lot by locating pedestrian access along one or both side lot lines. In this way, the spaces usually left over between houses take on multiple tasks, acting as both buffer and access. Four of the six lots share one path that moves through the block from street to alley to street, a clear reading of public accessibility through the depth of the block. In the other two lots, more traditional flag lot configurations, there are cautionary lessons as well. These are also organized with access along the edge of the lots, but the depth of public access is shallower, arriving only midway into the site. When one is at the sidewalk threshold, the spatial structure has depth, but the physical clues are less inviting. One is unsure whether one is welcome to move deeper into the site (figures 136 and 137).

In Horatio West, the position and orientation of the containing walls of the front rooms of each house organize the access to other units deeper in the site as well as provide privacy for each household. The site has several public-to-private thresholds—at the sidewalk, the entry patios, the courtyard, the rear entry patios, the archway, and the rear parking court. This depth is reinforced by natural light in the central and parking courtyards that bring both visitors and residents deeper into the site (figures 138 and 139).

In the last two examples, depth not only increases the density of units in the setting but also introduces additional levels and forms of access. A deeper structure holds greater variety and choice in ways of relating to the street, to neighbors, and to the landscape.

chapter eight

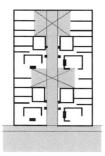

138. *Left:* Horatio West: diagram showing pedestrian and vehicular access moving through the full depth of the site.

139. *Right:* Full depth in Horatio West.

transformational potential of a fabric

Numerical definitions of density are static. They give a picture of or set a goal for density at one moment in time, failing to capture the temporal, changing character of dwelling—as both activity and physical setting. A morphological definition of density is a necessary complement in that it allows the designer to see and embed in a fabric the dynamics of choices in density. Then increases in density can also be achieved through ongoing transformations over time.

This is not a suggestion for predicting change but a call to recognize that every setting is reinterpreted and reused. Design that ignores the process or sees it as undesirable limits the long-term life of a place. Understanding that the nascent structure of every setting both limits and reveals the potential for additional building and use allows density to be designed. Again, the distinctions between an initially volumetric and a woven ordering lead to different kinds of physical additions and transformations in the setting (figure 140).

Levittown and Clayton, as exemplary volumetric settings, hold change in ways that are controlled by the shell of the house. In Levittown, affordability was achieved through the mass production of the house, not through a maximizing of density. At a time when construction costs were significantly more critical than land costs, building materials and room sizes were minimized. As a result, the lots themselves are dimensionally generous by present-day standards. The initial structure was established by a prototypical, inwardly focused house[6] positioned forward on its lot and to one side to accommodate car access along the side of the house.

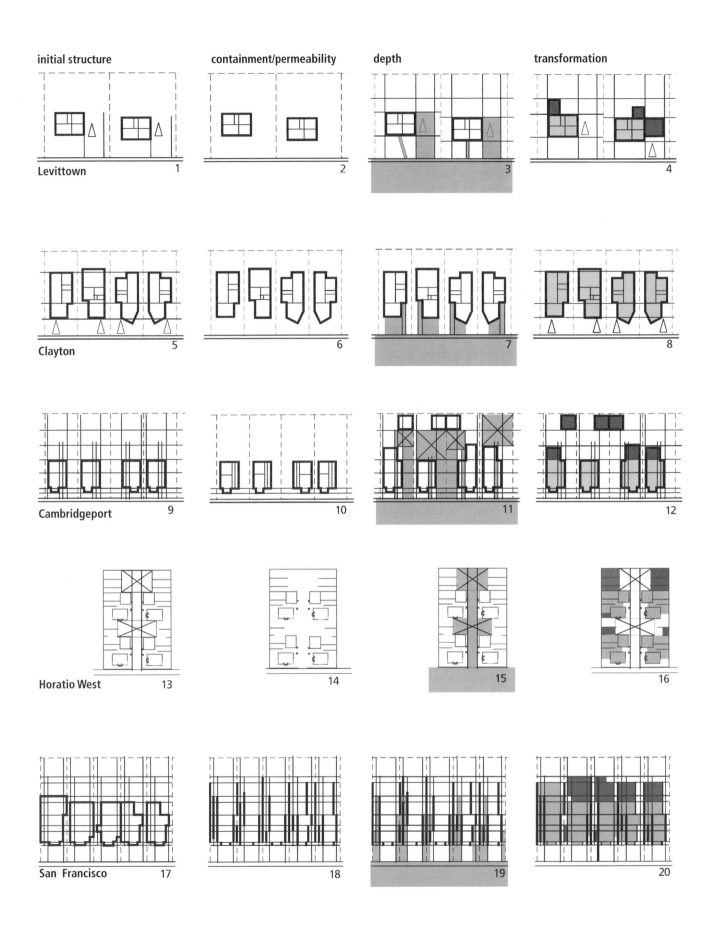

initial structure

containment/permeability

depth

transformation

Levittown 1

2

3

4

Clayton 5

6

7

8

Cambridgeport 9

10

11

12

Horatio West 13

14

15

16

San Francisco 17

18

19

20

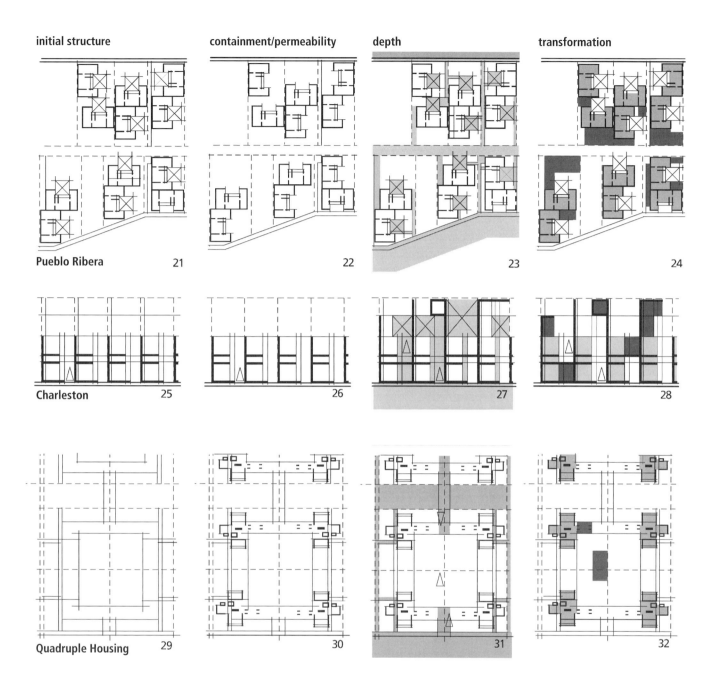

initial structure containment/permeability depth transformation

Pueblo Ribera 21 22 23 24

Charleston 25 26 27 28

Quadruple Housing 29 30 31 32

140. Comparing densities as structured settings.

The dimensional capacity of this initial structure at the lot level has supported an increase in density of building. The character of the additions is one of aggregation and attachment to the shell, reinforcing the centripetal nature of dwelling. As density increases, there is a shared pattern to the ways in which additions are made, with a great deal of individual variation in which the collective structure is still highly discernible. But the structure remains the same: the bounding volume of the house expands to fill the lot, intensifying the homogeneity and the residuum quality of the spaces between the houses.

141a, b. Levittown-like settings without capacity in the setting for growth.

Although Levittown has so often been used to caricature the suburbs, its capacity for transformation is much greater than that of many of the subsequent Levitt-like and contemporary communities that followed (figures 141a–b). In Clayton, where density has been significantly increased by packing the volumetric buildings in close proximity, dimensional capacity has been eliminated from the lot. The dimensions of the outdoor skirt are minimized: the length of a car determines the depth of the front yard, a small rear yard holds the outdoor barbecue, and a house is protected with a 5-foot yard. At a time when land costs have risen, the use of a lot is "maximized." Since its packed structuring does not have an intervening order to direct growth in the setting, transformations are more likely to be implemented on a house-by-house basis, as there is no larger pattern of settlement. There is very limited potential for change in the setting. Most of it is likely to occur inside the shells of the houses, with little effect on the density of the setting.

In their initial structure, Clayton and portions of Charleston have similar numerical measures of density, particularly the ratio of built area to land. Both case study settings have floor-area ratios (FARs)[7] of about .5. In the volumetric structuring of Clayton, the building footprint maximizes its occupancy of the site. As previously discussed, there is little room for change to increase density except by adding another floor. Extending the same numerical understanding of density to Charleston could lead to a conclusion that Charleston has the same limitations to change. Yet the fabric in Charleston has constantly undergone physical change through additions and subtractions built primarily in the depth of the lot. In the initial structure, the repetition and position of partially contained house forms build a fabric with open, ordered relations between the attributes of dimension, access, assembly, containment, and claim. None of them is singularly controlled by the perimeter of the house, but together they order the setting with permeability and depth (figures 142–146).

chapter eight

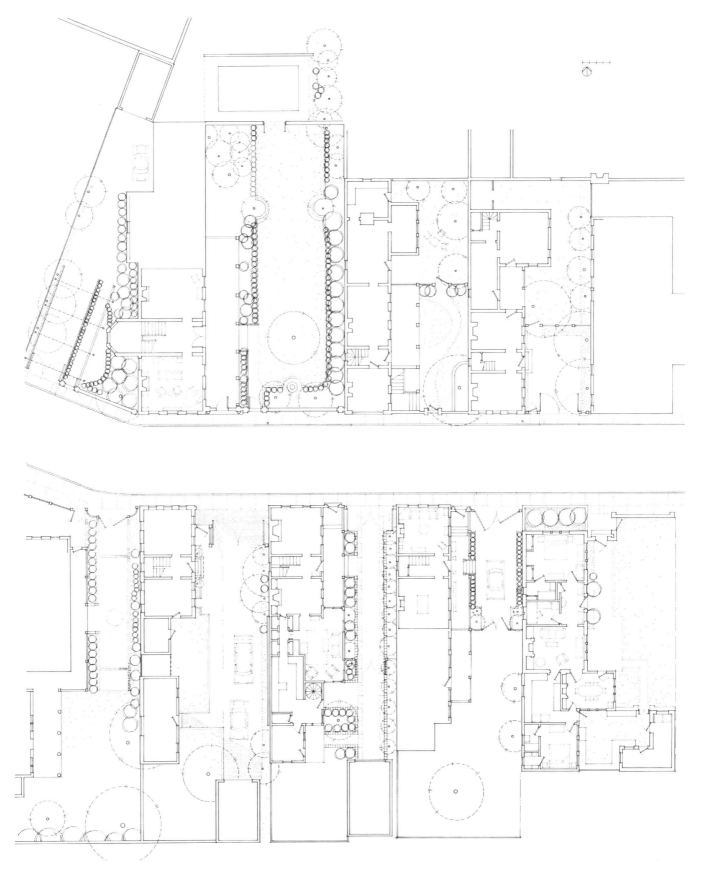

142. Charleston—inhabited.

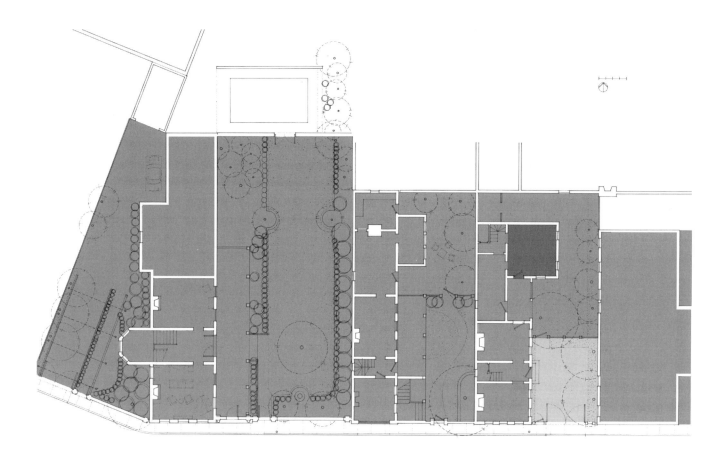

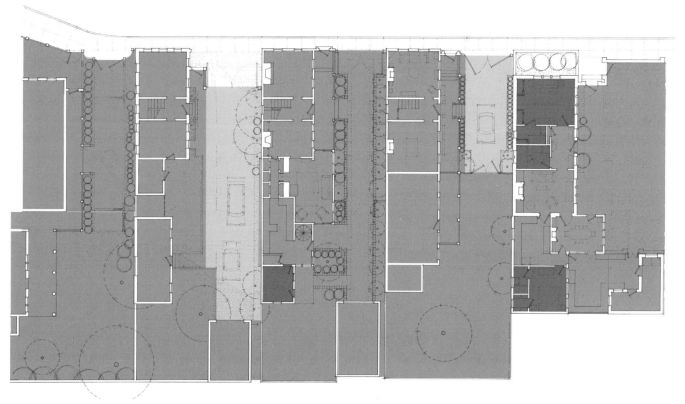

143. Charleston—claimed. In general, each lot in this Charleston setting is occupied by one household. But this setting also supports several unrelated households living on a single lot. Living space can be divided into front and back units or upper and lower units. When more than one household occupies each lot, neighbors share the side yard as access. Thus, in this plan, three side yards are toned as claimed by "neighbors," and the remaining side yards are claimed by "households."

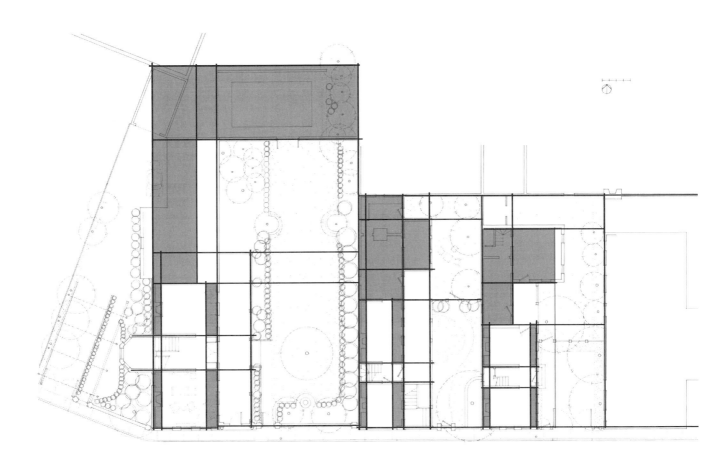

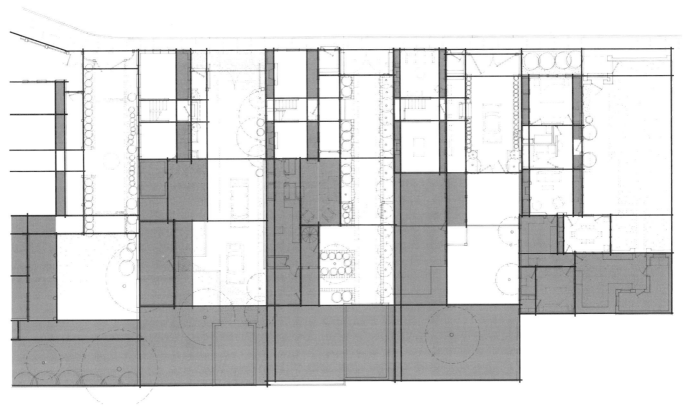

144. Charleston—dimensioned.

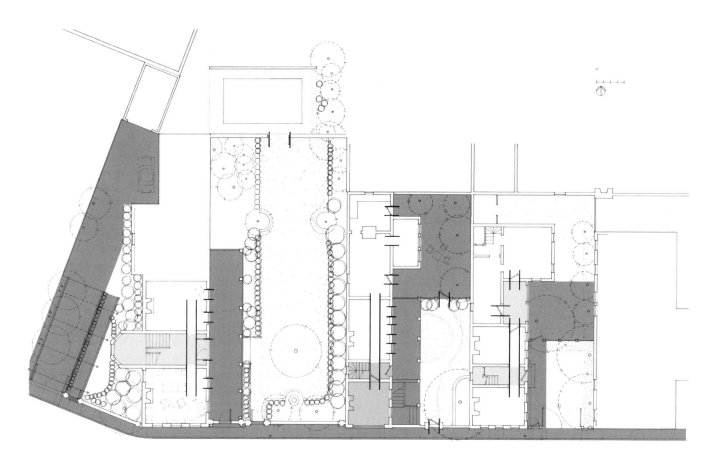

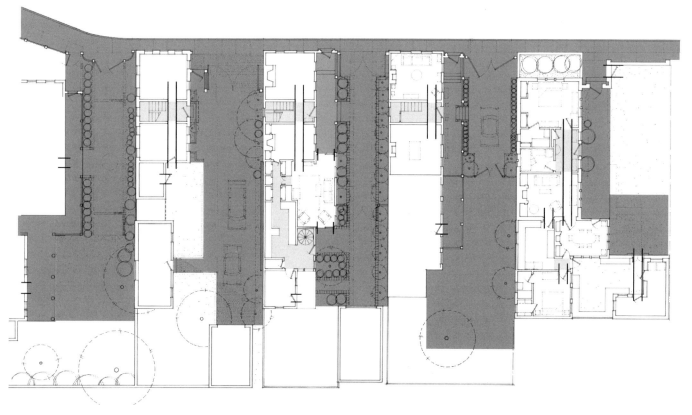

145. Charleston—accessed.

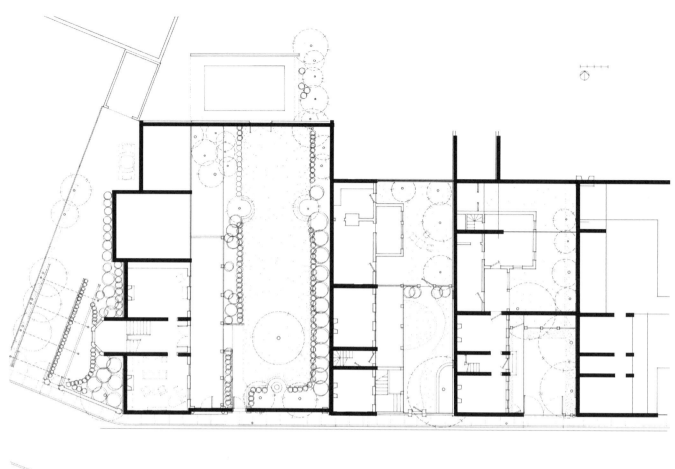

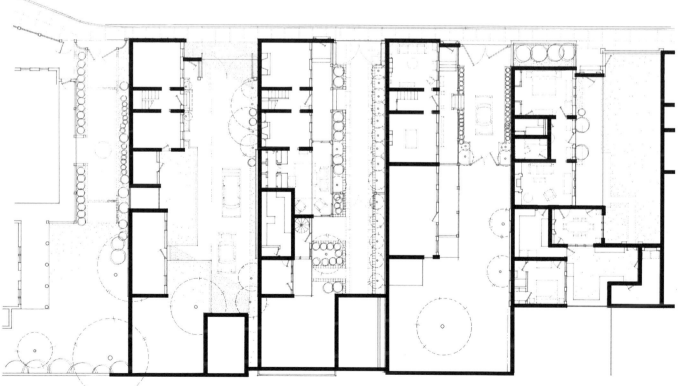

146. Charleston—contained.

As one moves along the streets of Charleston, one senses a steady rhythm of house and side yard that provides views into the depth of the site. As one moves through the front door and into the porch that sits between house and side yard, the direction of movement is again deeper into the site. Along the way, one can move into the house, move into the yard, or continue onward, arriving in a rear patio that organizes more activities around it. These may be the activities of one household, or the lot can collectively structure several households.[8] The initial structuring of the fabric and its potential for the extension of public access through the depth of the site are critical to informing transformations that maintain shared relations. The setting has increased in density through an increase in amount of building, mostly in the rear of the lot. The number of dwelling units has changed, increasing and decreasing as the dwelling on each lot is read as one family or more, as the front house is given to commercial use, or as the rear kitchen house becomes a bed-and-breakfast (figures 147a–b).

147a, b. Charleston—transformed.

In the debates over the next course of action for our suburbs, some present the decision as one between brownfield or greenfield, infill or sprawl. The reality is that choosing one will not preclude the other. Whether at the suburban fringe or the centers, we need to debate what else can be built. Proposing that we build fabrics as one alternative requires competence in seeing and designing systemic actions within a setting. This requires reading the topographic, physical, and social forms and patterns that exist prior to any building intervention, intensifying the existing qualities that make a place particular, and adding the qualities of a fabric, if missing.

The harder task in designing density is transforming a culture that sees the house as a commodity. The way we develop and produce housing is deeply rooted not only in the design culture but also in the consumer culture, economic systems, political policies, and manufacturing processes over which architects have little direct influence. Nonetheless, architects can and need to reinsert themselves into the debate about suburban housing, for the physical form of our settings is not insignificant.

In the long view of the history of settlement, seeing dwelling as a fabric is not new. It is a design tradition rooted in economic, political, and social systems that has produced the places we admire. In this long view, it is the suburb that is a new artifact. Bringing this discipline of the fabric to the suburbs transforms the way we think about detached housing. Rather than focusing on the object, seeing the fabric allows us to enter into the spaces of dwelling. In this way, our suburbs can be designed to do more: to support connections and social interactions with privacy; to accommodate diversity with sharing; and to provide outdoor spaces without waste. By weaving a fabric of dwelling, we not only can sustain living in the suburbs but transform it to support dwelling in ways as yet unforeseen.

For years now, architects have been providing outside instead of inside, but that is not their job at all; their job is to provide inside even if it happens to be outside.

ALDO VAN EYCK
as quoted in Peter Davey,
"Home-Making," *Architectural Review* 10 (1996)

notes

INTRODUCTION

1. Annual single-family housing starts have ranged between 1,029,900 and 1,270,800 units since 1992, according to data from the U.S. Census.

2. The notable exceptions are now well known as movements in suburban design: new urbanism and transit-oriented developments.

3. Claude Fischer, *The Urban Experience* (New York: Harcourt Brace Jovanovich, 1976), 204–233; Anne Vernez Moudon, "Urban Morphology as an Emerging Interdisciplinary Field," *Urban Morphology: Journal of the International Seminar on Urban Form* 1 (1997): 3–10.

4. See, for example, Leonardo Benevelo, *The History of the City* (London: Scolar Press, 1980).

5. Saverio Muratori, *Studi per una operante storia urbana di Venezia* (Rome: Istituto Poligrafico dello Stato P.V., 1959); Klaus Herdeg, *Formal Structure in Islamic Architecture of Iran and Turkistan* (New York: Rizzoli International Publications, 1990).

6. A full discussion of representation of fabrics is provided in chapter 4 of this book.

7. For example, Susan Kent, ed., *Method and Theory for Activity Area Research: An Ethnoarchaeological Approach* (New York: Columbia University Press, 1987).

8. For example, Paul Oliver, *Dwellings: The House across the World* (Austin: University of Texas Press, 1987).

9. Robert L. Vickery, *Anthrophysical Form: Two Families and Their Neighborhood Environments* (Charlottesville: University Press of Virginia, 1972).

10. Horacio Caminos, John Turner, and John Steffian, *Urban Dwelling Environments: An Elementary Survey of Settlements for the Study of Design Determinants* (Cambridge, Mass.: MIT Press, 1969).

11. For a detailed discussion of the design process, see Peter G. Rowe, *Design Thinking* (Cambridge, Mass: MIT Press, 1987).

12. N. John Habraken et al., *Variations: The Systematic Design of Supports* (Cambridge, Mass.: Laboratory of Architecture and Planning, MIT, 1976); N. John Habraken, *The Structure of the Ordinary: Form and Control in the Built Environment* (Cambridge, Mass.: MIT Press, 1998); Bill Hillier et al., "Natural Movement: Or, Configuration and Attraction in Urban Pedestrian Movement," *Environment and Planning B: Planning and Design* 20 (1993): 29–66; Bill Hillier, "Against Enclosure," in *Rehumanizing Housing,* Necdet Teymur, Thomas Markus, and Tom Woolley, eds. (London: Butterworths, 1988), 63–88; Richard C. MacCormac, "The Anatomy of Wright's Aesthetic," in *Writings on Wright: Selected Comment on Frank Lloyd Wright,* H. Allen Brooks, ed. (Cambridge, Mass.: MIT Press, 1981), 161–188; Stanford Anderson, "Studies toward an Ecological Model of the Urban Environment," in *On Streets,* Stanford Anderson, ed. (Cambridge, Mass: MIT Press, 1978).

CHAPTER ONE: BEGINNINGS OF A PRODUCTION SYSTEM

1. The Horatio West Court Apartments are located in Santa Monica, California. They were designed by Irving Gill and built in 1919.

2. H. Allen Brooks, "Wright and the Destruction of the Box," in *Writings on Wright: Selected Comment on Frank Lloyd Wright,* H. Allen Brooks, ed. (Cambridge, Mass.: MIT Press, 1981), 174–188.

3. Yukio Futagawa, ed., *Frank Lloyd Wright Monographs 1902–1906* (Tokyo: A.D.A. Edita, 1987), vol. 2. In 1900, Wright proposed the first of many versions of his quadruple block plan. The scheme was further developed as a project for Charles E. Roberts in Oak Park, Illinois, in 1903. It took on its most famed and dispersed version in Broadacre City in 1932 and was finally executed in its most compact form as the Suntop Homes in 1939.

4. Futagawa, *Frank Lloyd Wright Monographs,* vol. 1, 154–155.

5. In Wright's various versions of the early quadruple block plans, the lot size was about 87 feet by 81 feet, or 7,047 square feet. This is about 6.2 units per acre, compared to the single unit per acre of Broadacre City. It is also interesting to compare this with later Levittown lots that are 60 feet by 100 feet, or 7.26 units per acre.

6. Both the hierarchy and the separation of vehicular and pedestrian access have been much imitated as well as critiqued. Jane Jacobs, *The Death and Life of Great American Cities* (New York: Random House, 1961), saw the specialization of streets for vehicular functions as dehumanizing, stripping the street of its potential for human interaction. Also, the hierarchy of roadways arrayed around superblocks decreased the number of routes and therefore choices by which residents could move in, out, and through their neighborhoods. This lack of alternatives leads to congestion at particular times of the day.

7. Residents who have lived in Radburn for many years—as well as those who have returned to rear their own families—refer to their yards as the "path-side" or "car-side."

8. Based on my own informal survey of some twenty-four residents in 1992.

9. Clarence S. Stein, *Toward New Towns for America*, 6th ed. (Cambridge, Mass.: MIT Press, 1978), 228–248.

10. Historic American Buildings Survey, *The Horatio West Court Apartments*, Survey No. CAL 1930 (Washington, D.C.: U.S. National Park Service, 1968), 1. Also, Esther McCoy, *Five California Architects* (New York: Praeger Publishers, 1975), 85–87, describes the various projects in which Gill explored economy and design.

11. Herbert Gans, *The Levittowners: Ways of Life and Politics in a New Suburban Community* (New York: Pantheon, 1967).

12. Barbara Kelly, *Expanding the American Dream: Building and Rebuilding Levittown* (Albany: State University of New York Press, 1993), described how even the developer recognized the lack of connection and access to the backyard. In subsequent model homes, the plan of the house is reoriented 90 degrees so that the living room and dining room are parallel to the drive and perpendicular to the street.

13. "Up from the Potato Fields," *Time*, July 3, 1950, 69.

14. Harold Wattel, "Levittown: A Suburban Community," in *The Suburban Community*, William M. Dobriner, ed. (New York: G. P. Putnam's Sons, 1958).

CHAPTER TWO: PERSISTENCE OF THE BOX

1. The long history of pattern books and model homes is traced by Gwendolyn Wright in *Building the Dream: A Social History of Housing in America* (Cambridge, Mass.: MIT Press, 1981), 73–75.

2. See, for example, John Keats, *The Crack in the Picture Window* (Boston: Houghton Mifflin, 1956); and William Whyte, *The Organization Man* (Garden City, N.J.: Doubleday Anchor, 1956).

3. Lewis Mumford, *The City in History: Its Origins, Its Transformations, and Its Prospects* (New York: Harcourt, Brace and World, 1961), 486.

4. "Little Boxes" was written by Malvina Reynolds in 1963 and sung by Pete Seeger.

5. Most noted of the work of that period are Bennett Berger, *Working Class Suburbs* (Berkeley: University of California Press, 1960); William M. Dobriner, *Class in Suburbia* (Englewood Cliffs, N.J.: Prentice Hall, 1963); Herbert Gans, *The Levittowners: Ways of Life and Politics in a New Suburban Community* (New York: Pantheon, 1967); and Scott Donaldson, *The Suburban Myth* (New York: Columbia University Press, 1969).

6. Based upon my own survey of Radburn residents in 1991.

7. Jane Jacobs, *The Death and Life of Great American Cities* (New York: Random House, 1961).

8. Kenneth Jackson, *The Crabgrass Frontier: The Suburbanization of the United States* (New York: Oxford University Press, 1985), 272.

9. For example, Peter Calthorpe, *The Next American Metropolis: Ecology, Community, and the American Dream* (New York: Princeton Architectural Press, 1993); Cynthia Girling and Kenneth Helphand, *Yard, Street, Park: The Design of Suburban Open Space* (New York: John Wiley and Sons, 1994).

10. Jackson, *Crabgrass Frontier*, 279.

11. For example, Dick Rosenberg et al., *Beyond Sprawl: New Patterns of Growth to Fit the New California* (San Francisco: Bank of America et al., 1995); Mark Baldassare, *Trouble in Paradise: The Suburban Transformation in America* (New York: Columbia University Press, 1986).

CHAPTER THREE: DEFINING DWELLING

1. Herman Hertzberger, *Lessons for Students in Architecture* (Rotterdam: Uitgeverij, 1991), 150.

2. Mary C. Waters, *Ethnic Options: Choosing Identities in America* (Berkeley: University of California Press, 1990), describes how we construct our cultural practices and the influences on the choices we make.

3. Edward T. Hall, in his pioneering work *The Hidden Dimension* (Garden City, N.Y.: Doubleday, 1966), describes how differences in culture predispose us to read the environment in different ways—how a door ajar can be understood as welcoming by some and as a request for privacy by others.

4. For example, Peter Calthorpe, *The Next American Metropolis: Ecology, Community, and the American Dream* (New York: Princeton Architectural Press, 1993), describes the demographic shift of the last twenty years: shrinking family size and increasing percentages of singles, single-parent families, two-income families, and people older than sixty-five. In a similar vein, the images of household have been questioned by many—for example, by Mark Robbins, curator of the Wexner Center exhibit "House Rules," as reported by Akiko Busch in "Suburbia and Suspense," *Metropolis* 14 (October 1994): 116, and by Kenneth Jackson, *The Crabgrass Frontier: The Suburbanization of the United States* (New York: Oxford University Press, 1985).

5. For further examples of such definitions, see Anne Vernez Moudon, "Urban Morphology as an Emerging Interdisciplinary Field," *Urban Morphology: Journal of the International Seminar on Urban Form* 1 (1997): 3–10; N. John Habraken, "The Control of Complexity," *Places* 4 (1987): 3–15.

6. For instance, see James Short, ed., *The Social Fabric of the Metropolis: Contributions of the Chicago School of Urban Sociology* (Chicago: University of Chicago Press, 1971), as well Elizabeth Moule and Stefanos Polyzoides, "The Street, the Block and the Building," in *The New Urbanism: Toward an Architecture of Community*, Peter Katz, ed. (New York: McGraw-Hill, 1994); the earliest reference I have found for this use of the word is in Shakespeare:

> . . . These our actors,
> As I foretold you, were all spirits, and
> Are melted into air, into thin air;
> And, like the baseless fabric of this vision,
> The cloud-capp'd towers, the gorgeous palaces,
> The solemn temples, the great globe itself,
> Yea, all which it inherit, shall dissolve,
> And, like this insubstantial pageant faded,
> Leave not a rack behind.

(*Tempest* 4.1.151–159)

1. Peter G. Rowe, *Design Thinking* (Cambridge, Mass.: MIT Press, 1987), 97–100, describes the influence of representation to reveal and conceal aspects for design consideration.

2. Although the propositions about representation in this chapter are illustrated through plans, the argument extends to other two-dimensional drawings such as sections, as well as three-dimensional representations such as modeling.

3. Camillo Sitte, *The Art of Building Cities: City Building According to Its Artistic Fundamentals* (New York: Reinhold Publishing, 1945).

4. N. John Habraken, *SAR '73: The Methodical Formulations of Agreements Concerning the Direct Dwelling Environment* (Eindhoven, the Netherlands: Stichting Architekten Research, 1973).

5. Sanborn Map Company, Special Services Division, *Sanborn Services for City and Regional Planners* (Chicago: Sanborn Map Company, 1957).

6. Anne Vernez Moudon, *Built for Change: Neighborhood Architecture in San Francisco* (Cambridge, Mass.: MIT Press, 1986).

7. Horacio Caminos, John Turner, and John Steffian, *Urban Dwelling Environments: An Elementary Survey of Settlements for the Study of Design Determinants* (Cambridge, Mass.: MIT Press, 1969).

8. Klaus Herdeg, *Formal Structure in Islamic Architecture of Iran and Turkistan* (New York: Rizzoli International Publications, 1990).

9. Habraken, *SAR '73.*

10. Anne Vernez Moudon, "Getting to Know the Built Landscape: Typomorphology," in *Ordering Space: Types in Architecture and Design,* Karen A. Franck and Lynda H. Schneekloth, eds. (New York: Van Nostrand Reinhold, 1994), 291, describes Gianfranco Caniggia's hierarchy in four scales: the building *(edificio),* the group of buildings *(tessuto* or building fabric), the city *(città),* and the region *(territorio).*

11. Caminos et al., *Urban Dwelling Environments,* v.

12. Saverio Muratori, *Studi per una operante storia urbana di Venezia* (Rome: Istituto Poligrafico dello Stato P.V., 1959).

13. Stanford Anderson, "People in the Physical Environment: The Urban Ecology of Streets," in *On Streets,* Stanford Anderson, ed. (Cambridge, Mass.: MIT Press, 1978), 1–11.

14. For example, Susan Kent, *Analyzing Activity Areas: An Ethno-archaeological Study of the Use of Space* (Albuquerque: University of New Mexico Press, 1984).

15. For example, Paul Oliver, *Dwellings: The House across the World* (Austin: University of Texas Press, 1987).

16. To ensure this dual use, parallel studies were conducted using the representation both for analysis and in projection. The conventions of the representation were modified through a reiterative process of field documentation, case study analysis, and design projection.

17. The Sachs Apartments (formerly Manola Courts) were designed by Rudolf M. Schindler in 1928.

18. For a description of Levittown, see chapter 1 of this book.

19. These were determined through a detailed analysis of sizes of activities. A wide array of residential activities was defined, from talking on the phone to entertaining two to twelve guests. Both a range and normative sizes were determined for each activity, and these areas were then logged onto a chart. As a result of this mapping, activities were classified into these two broad groups, primary and personal.

20. Lateral loading in the assemblage of residential fabrics is discussed in chapter 7, "Unpacking."

21. The concept of partial containment is used here as described by Maurice K. Smith, professor emeritus of the Department of Architecture at Massachusetts Institute of Technology.

CHAPTER FIVE: ACCOMMODATING CHOICE

1. "House Rules" was an exhibit held at the Wexner Center in 1994, curated by Mark Robbins.

2. Quoted in Akiko Busch, "Suburbia and Suspense," *Metropolis* 14 (October 1994): 116.

3. Amos Rapoport, "Foreword," in *Housing, Culture, and Design: A Comparative Perspective*, Setha Low and Erve Chambers, eds. (Philadelphia: University of Pennsylvania Press, 1989), xvii, talks of "congruence" between lifestyle and the environment. Ellen J. Pader, "Spatiality and Social Change: Domestic Space Use in Mexico and the United States," *American Ethnologist* 20 (1993): 114, writes that "the ways in which people use and organize their spaces are dynamically implicated in the enculturation process, in the creation, maintenance, and transformation of one's 'intelligible universe.'"

4. This story is based upon an interview that I conducted in the spring of 1995. The family name is changed.

5. This "central" reading of a predominantly linear house form occurs frequently in San Francisco houses. Other examples will be discussed later in the chapter.

6. This story is based on interviews that I conducted in the spring of 1996. The family name is changed.

7. Many architects discuss the concept of capacity and the phenomenon of form's ability to take on multiple uses. Some key sources are N. John Habraken, "The Control of Complexity," *Places* 4 (1987): 3–15, who discusses the concept of capacity at many environmental levels; Stanford Anderson, "People in the Physical Environment: The Urban Ecology of Streets," in *On Streets*, Stanford Anderson, ed. (Cambridge, Mass.: MIT Press, 1978), who describes capacity as an environmental latency; Herman Hertzberger, *Lessons for Students in Architecture* (Rotterdam: Uitgeverij, 1991), who describes the polyvalent nature of form to be "read" or used in a variety of ways, depending upon what the individual brings as an association; and Robert Venturi, "Contradictory Levels Continued: The Double-Functioning Element," in *Complexity and Contradiction in Architecture* (New York: Museum of Modern Art, 1977), who questions multifunctioning flexibility—a "both-and" problem—and advocates for the double-functioning element.

8. The relationship between access and use as a support for choice is discussed at the house and planning levels by Ellen J. Pader and Bill Hillier. Pader, in "Spatiality and Social Change," describes the circulation and organization of rooms as key in establishing familism in Mexican society and contrasts forms of circulation in Mexican houses and U.S. homes. Bill Hillier et al., in "Natural Movement: Or, Configuration and Attraction in Urban Pedestrian Movement," *Environment and Planning B: Planning and Design* 20 (1993): 29–66, makes the case against hierarchic forms of access that emphasize "to and from" attraction theories and advocates for more multiple forms of urban movement that allow greater degrees of choice.

9. Roderick J. Lawrence, *Housing, Dwellings and Homes: Design Theory, Research and Practice* (Chichester, England: John Wiley and Sons, 1987), describes research in housing choices in relation to privacy and territoriality. Klaus Herdeg, *Formal Structure in Islamic Architecture of Iran and Turkistan* (New York: Rizzoli International Publications, 1990), graphically depicts the overlapping domains of a city fabric as experienced by people of various social and religious positions. And Anderson, in "People in the Physical Environment," graphically maps

a public-to-private gradient of claim over the fabric of Paris to study the potential reading of spaces. The term *territorial claim* is also used to describe the process of controlling a space. To increase possibilities for choice, the terms need to be uncoupled because the claim over a territory could be part of choice, changing on a day-to-day basis or from resident to resident. Therefore, *territory* refers to the space and *claim* refers to the control of activity.

10. In this study, the capacity of a house to hold a variety of activities is identified by comparing two sources of dimensions. The first is a set of dimensional standards for activities derived from American standards books. The second is field documentation and standards from other countries. In each setting, the area of primary activities for a household is compared to the normative standards. Other arrangements for the same activity are compared to the highlighted area. Then the areas of additional activities, if any, selected by residents are identified. These territories are toned, and their dimensions are also compared to normative standards. Other places of personalization as shown by personal effects are also toned. The resulting map is then analyzed as to the structuring of primary and personal activities in relation to dimensions.

11. One model counters the effects of the service structure by extending a long kitchen parallel with the garage, another by adding an optional study or guest bedroom.

12. In San Francisco, half-baths have often been added in the zone of the stairs. This change is supported by the dimensional capacity in the setting, not by the assembled capacity. In this case, the service walls run perpendicular to the bearing walls—a necessity given the narrowness of the space. Also, in the second house from the left in figure 91, most of the service walls were added perpendicular to the bearing walls. This shift occurred in a later renovation that used the house's capacity when subdividing the house into five units. The new service walls now more permanently subdivide the house, decreasing the capacity for subsequent change without substantial demolition.

13. In a separate study that I conducted with students at the University of California, Berkeley, the prior homes and the patterns of dwelling of immigrant populations from Mexico and China were compared to American housing patterns. This conclusion is supported by the work of Susan Kent, *Analyzing Activity Areas: An Ethnoarchaeological Study of the Use of Space* (Albuquerque: University of New Mexico Press, 1984); Christopher Wilson, "When a Room Is the Hall," *Mass: Journal of the School of Architecture and Planning, University of New Mexico* 2 (Summer 1984): 17–23; and Pader, "Spatiality and Social Change."

14. Stefan Pikusa, in "Designing for Functional Adaptation: A Lesson from History," *Architecture Australia* 72 (1983): 62–67, shows how the size and shape of spaces can have a bearing on whether a room can serve different purposes. He argues for giving an occupant choice through intentional ambiguity.

CHAPTER SIX: SHARING IN A SETTING

1. One manifestation of this resurgence can be found just in the number of publications in the last decade that use the term *community* in their titles: for instance, Peter Calthorpe, *The Next American Metropolis: Ecology, Community, and the American Dream* (New York: Princeton Architectural Press, 1993); Peter Katz, *The New Urbanism: Toward an Architecture of Community* (New York: McGraw-Hill, 1994); and Richard Moe and Carter Wilkie, *Changing Places: Rebuilding Community in the Age of Sprawl* (New York: Henry Holt, 1997).

2. This conclusion is based upon interviews with residents that I conducted in 1991.

3. N. John Habraken describes type as a shared understanding in *The Appearance of the Form: Four Essays on the Position Designing Takes between People and Things*, 2d ed. (Cambridge, Mass.: Awater Press, 1988).

4. Cambridge Historical Commission, *Survey of Architectural History in Cambridge*, vol. 3, *Cambridgeport* (Cambridge, Mass.: MIT Press, 1971), 37.

5. Beware the false connector. Although some bemoan the loss of the front porch as a symbol of the decline of community or insist upon it as a way to mimic the image of neighborhood, a porch alone does not ensure sharing through connection. To insist that houses in Minnesota, laden with summer mosquitoes and winter ice, have front porches to nurture community limits times when sharing can take place. A porch that serves as a transition between a bedroom and the street also makes no sense but is not unusual when porches are applied only from the perspective of the streetscape. Territories of sharing need to connect one space and its activities with another. Rather than appropriating icons of territorial sharing, spatial sharing can take on a variety of forms that are structured in a setting.

6. There is a dearth of words to describe personal, transitional spaces. Most find their roots in the Victorian architecture of the types under discussion—bay window, entry vestibules, alcoves. The kinds of space in the interior edge zones of the Sachs Apartments have no ready vocabulary.

7. According to Judith Sheine, resident of the Sachs Apartments and chronicler of Schindler's practice, the complex we now call the Sachs Apartments was built over a period of time and not all at once. The upper and lower central buildings were built in 1926 for Herman Sachs, with home and gallery on the top level of the upper building and painting studio and guest room on the lower levels. The three lower apartments were also built at the time of the house. To the west are buildings that Schindler renovated in the 1920s and 1930s. In 1939, Schindler designed the block of apartments on the upper portion of the site, to the east of the Sachs studio and home.

CHAPTER SEVEN: UNPACKING

1. A succinct summary of these issues is provided in Harold M. Proshansky, William Ittelson, and Leanne Rivlin, "Freedom of Choice and Behavior in the Physical Setting," *Environmental Psychology: Man and His Physical Setting*, Harold M. Proshansky, William Ittleson, and Leanne Rivlin, eds. (New York: Holt, Rinehart and Winston, 1970).

2. Access in Clayton between the street and house can be described as continuous from the viewpoint of each resident arriving at his or her home by car. The sequence then is quite similar to San Francisco in that the access moves directly from the street through the garage and into the house, squeezing by or through the bath and laundry.

3. The use of this term was introduced in chapter 4.

4. These wood frame walls are reminiscent of the concrete frames in Schindler's Lovell Beach house.

5. House for two families, Rudolf and Pauline Schindler and Marian and Clyde Chace, in West Hollywood, California.

6. Originally designed as vacation houses in La Jolla, California, for W. L. Lloyd.

7. By 1980, one pair of contiguous units had been converted into a one-family house.

8. Charleston blocks are substantially longer in the north-south direction than in the east-west direction. As a result, a majority of the houses are oriented to the south. The atypical houses on the east-west streets tend to be open to the west, although there is less consistency in this direction.

9. The Horatio West Court Apartments were introduced in chapter 1.

1. These approaches are described by James Wentling and Lloyd Bookout, eds., *Density by Design* (Washington, D.C.: Urban Land Institute, 1988); Walter Richardson, "Designing High Density Single Family Housing: Variation on the Zero Lot Line Theme," *Urban Land* 47 (February 1988): 15–20; and David Jensen Associates, Inc., and the National Association of Home Builders, *Small Lots — Big Savings* (Washington, D.C.: NAHB, 1986).

2. Jack Chang, "Concord Embraces Tight Infill Housing," *Contra Costa Times*, September 3, 2000, 16.

3. For a thorough examination of the definitions of perceived and measured density in relation to dwelling types, see Ernest R. Alexander, "Density Measures: A Review and Analysis," *Journal of Architectural and Planning Research* 10 (Autumn 1993): 181–202.

4. N. John Habraken, *The Structure of the Ordinary: Form and Control in the Built Environment* (Cambridge, Mass.: MIT Press, 1998), describes this phenomenon of every place holding other places as "included territories" and the perception of thresholds as "territorial depth."

5. The depth of a setting is, of course, integrally linked to issues of planning and decisions regarding block size, network, and infrastructural relations, although these topics are beyond the scope of discussion here.

6. In the initial design of the Levittown house, the developers were keenly aware of the small size of the house and anticipated that the residents would make changes. Levitt assumed that expansion would be necessary and that, when extra space was needed, the residents would take the space under the roof. Despite the developer's intention, the form of the original Cape Cod house did not hold this potential for change. Anyone who has tried to renovate an attic space in which the rafters sit directly on the top plate of the floor below knows that the usable clear height in such a space is much less than the implied volume and that light is limited to the gable ends. The habitable space under the gable is small, narrow, and relatively dark. Most residents who built a second floor chose to rebuild the roof entirely. Much of the increase in density has been through first-floor additions, most readily achieved by extending the length of the house in the gable direction and secondarily by increasing the depth of the house.

7. FAR is the ratio between the gross floor area of a building, all floors, and the total area of a site.

8. The Charleston single house has a long and interesting social history—a history some would argue makes the use of this house type questionable. The single house emerged in the late eighteenth century as a multistory building that was one room wide and three bays deep, including a central entrance and stair hall. Beyond the single house was the kitchen house, separated from the house for fire safety and above which lived the slaves. Other outbuildings, including carriage houses, were erected deep within the lot. Arguments against the use of this type because of its history miss the critical lessons of the potential of a setting to successfully hold transformation and change.

bibliography

Alexander, Ernest R. "Density Measures: A Review and Analysis." *Journal of Architectural and Planning Research* 10 (Autumn 1993): 181–202.

Alofsin, Anthony. "Broadacre City: The Reception of a Modernist Vision, 1932–1988." *Center: Modernist Visions and the Contemporary American City* 5 (1989): 8–43.

Altman, Irwin. "Privacy: A Conceptual Analysis." *Environment and Behavior* 8 (1976): 7–30.

———. *Culture and Environment.* Cambridge, England: Cambridge University Press, 1984.

Anderson, Stanford. "People in the Physical Environment: The Urban Ecology of Streets." In *On Streets*, edited by Stanford Anderson, 1–11. Cambridge, Mass.: MIT Press, 1978.

———. "Studies toward an Ecological Model of the Urban Environment." In *On Streets*, edited by Stanford Anderson, 267–308. Cambridge, Mass.: MIT Press, 1978.

Baldassare, Mark. *Trouble in Paradise: The Suburban Transformation in America.* New York: Columbia University Press, 1986.

Baudrillard, Jean. "The System of Objects." In *Design after Modernism: Beyond the Object*, edited by John Thackara, 171–182. Gloucester, England: Thames and Hudson, 1988.

Benevelo, Leonardo. *The History of the City.* London: Scolar Press, 1980.

Benjamin, David N., ed. *The Home: Words, Interpretations, Meanings and Environments.* Aldershot, England: Avebury, 1995.

Berger, Bennett. *Working Class Suburbs.* Berkeley: University of California Press, 1960.

Boles, Daralice. "Affordable Housing." *Progressive Architecture* 68 (February 1987): 86–91.

———. "Reordering the Suburbs." *Progressive Architecture* 70 (May 1989): 78–91.

Bourdieu, Pierre. *The Logic of Practice.* Stanford, Calif.: Stanford University Press, 1990.

Bressi, Todd. "Planning the American Dream." In *The New Urbanism: Toward an Architecture of Community,* edited by Peter Katz, xxv–xlii. New York: McGraw-Hill, 1994.

Brooks, H. Allen. "Wright and the Destruction of the Box." In *Writings on Wright: Selected Comment on Frank Lloyd Wright,* edited by H. Allen Brooks, 175–188. Cambridge, Mass.: MIT Press, 1981.

Buchanan, Peter, Liane Lefaivre, and Alexander Tzonis. *Aldo and Hannie van Eyck: Recent Work: Two = Twee.* Amsterdam: Stichting de Beurs van Berlage, 1989.

Busch, Akiko. "Suburbia and Suspense." *Metropolis* 14 (October 1994): 116–123.

Calthorpe, Peter. *The Next American Metropolis: Ecology, Community, and the American Dream.* New York: Princeton Architectural Press, 1993.

Cambridge Historical Commission. *Survey of Architectural History in Cambridge.* Vol. 3, *Cambridgeport.* Cambridge, Mass.: MIT Press, 1971.

Caminos, Horacio, John Turner, and John Steffian. *Urban Dwelling Environments: An Elementary Survey of Settlements for the Study of Design Determinants.* Cambridge, Mass.: MIT Press, 1969.

Canada Mortgage and Housing Corporation and Société Canadienne d'Hyotheques et de Logement. "Working Paper Two: The Evolution of the Housing Production Process." In *The Housing Industry: Perspective and Prospective,* edited by Canada Mortgage and Housing Corporation, 3–22. Rep. No. 6195. Ottawa, Ontario: CMHC, 1989.

Chang, Jack. "Concord Embraces Tight Infill Housing." *Contra Costa Times,* September 3, 2000, 16.

Chastain, Thomas, and Renee Chow. "Observations of Turfan." *Places* 4 (1987): 21–32.

Chermayeff, Serge, and Christopher Alexander. *Community and Privacy: Toward a New Architecture of Humanism.* Garden City, N.Y.: Doubleday, 1963.

Chermayeff, Serge, and Alexander Tzonis. *Shape of Community: Realization of Human Potential.* Harmondsworth, England: Penguin Books, 1971.

Chow, Renee Y. "Sharing in a Setting." *Places* 11 (1997): 64–65.

———. "House Form and Choice." *Traditional Dwellings and Settlements Review* 9 (1998): 51–61.

Christensen, Carol A. *The American Garden City and the Newtowns Movement.* Ann Arbor, Mich.: UMI Research Press, 1986.

Clark, Clifford E., Jr. *The American Family Home, 1800–1960.* Chapel Hill: University of North Carolina Press, 1986.

Conzen, Michael P., ed. *The Making of the American Landscape.* Boston: Unwin Hyman, 1990.

Craig, Lois. "Suburbs." *Design Quarterly* 132 (1986): 1–33.

Cummings, Abbott L. *The Framed Houses of Massachusetts Bay, 1625–1675.* Cambridge, Mass.: Belknap Press, 1979.

Davey, Peter. "Sustainable Suburbia." *Architectural Review* 198 (November 1995): 4–5.

———. "Home-Making." *Architectural Review* 200 (October 1996): 4–5.

David Jensen Associates, Inc., and the National Association of Home Builders. *Small Lots—Big Savings.* Washington, D.C.: NAHB, 1986.

Dennis, Michael. *Court and Garden: From the French Hotel to the City of Modern Architecture.* Cambridge, Mass.: MIT Press, 1986.

Dobriner, William M. *Class in Suburbia.* Englewood Cliffs, N.J.: Prentice Hall, 1963.

———, ed. *The Suburban Community.* New York: G. P. Putnam's Sons, 1958.

Donaldson, Scott. *The Suburban Myth.* New York: Columbia University Press, 1969.

Downing, Anthony J. *The Architecture of Country Houses.* New York: D. Appleton, 1850.

Duany, Andres. "Traditional Towns." *Architectural Design* 59 (1989): 60–64.

Evans, Robin. *Translations from Drawing to Building and Other Essays.* Cambridge, Mass.: MIT Press, 1997.

Fischer, Claude. *The Urban Experience.* New York: Harcourt Brace Jovanovich, 1976.

Fishman, Robert. *Bourgeois Utopias: The Rise and Fall of Suburbia.* New York: Basic Books, 1987.

Franck, Karen A., and Sherry Ahrentzen, eds. *New Households, New Housing.* New York: Van Nostrand Reinhold, 1994.

Futagawa, Yukio, ed. *Frank Lloyd Wright Monographs 1902–1906.* Tokyo: A.D.A. Edita, 1987.

Gans, Herbert. *The Levittowners: Ways of Life and Politics in a New Suburban Community.* New York: Pantheon, 1967.

Garreau, Joel. *Edge City: Life on the New Frontier.* New York: Doubleday, 1991.

Giedion, Sigfried. *Mechanization Takes Command: A Contribution to Anonymous History.* New York: Praeger, 1969.

Girling, Cynthia. "The Pedestrian Pocket: Reorienting Radburn." *Landscape Journal* 12 (1993): 40–50.

Girling, Cynthia, and Kenneth Helphand. *Yard, Street, Park: The Design of Suburban Open Space.* New York: John Wiley and Sons, 1994.

Glassie, Henry. *Folk Housing in Middle Virginia: A Structural Analysis of Historic Artifacts.* Knoxville: University of Tennessee Press, 1975.

Goode, Erica. "How Culture Molds Habits of Thought." *New York Times,* August 8, 2000, D1.

Goodman, Nelson. *Ways of Worldmaking.* Indianapolis: Hackett, 1978.

Gowans, Alan. *The Comfortable House: North American Suburban Architecture, 1890–1930.* Cambridge, Mass.: MIT Press, 1986.

Habraken, N. John. *Supports: An Alternative to Mass Housing.* London: Architectural Press, 1972 [1961 in Dutch]).

———. *SAR '73: The Methodical Formulations of Agreements Concerning the Direct Dwelling Environment.* Eindhoven, the Netherlands: Stichting Architekten Research, 1973.

———. *The Grunsfeld Variations: A Report on the Thematic Development of an Urban Tissue.* Cambridge, Mass.: MIT Department of Architecture, 1981.

———. "The Control of Complexity." *Places* 4 (1987): 3–15.

———. *The Appearance of the Form: Four Essays on the Position Designing Takes between People and Things.* 2d ed. Cambridge, Mass.: Awater Press, 1988.

———. *Transformations of the Site.* 3d ed. Cambridge, Mass.: Awater Press, 1988.

———. "Cultivating the Field: About an Attitude When Making Architecture." *Places* 9 (1996): 8–20.

———. *The Structure of the Ordinary: Form and Control in the Built Environment.* Cambridge, Mass.: MIT Press, 1998.

Habraken, N. John, J.T. Boekholt, P. Dinjens, and A.P. Thijssen. *Variations: The Systematic Design of Supports.* Cambridge, Mass.: Laboratory of Architecture and Planning, MIT, 1976.

Haizlip, Shirlee T. *The Sweeter the Juice.* New York: Simon and Schuster, 1994.

Hall, Edward T. *The Hidden Dimension.* Garden City, N.Y.: Doubleday, 1966.

———. "The Anthropology of Space: An Organizing Model." In *Environmental Psychology: Man and His Physical Setting,* edited by Harold M. Proshansky, William Ittelson, and Leanne Rivlin. New York: Holt, Rinehart and Winston, 1970.

Hayden, Dolores. *The Grand Domestic Revolution: A History of Feminist Designs for American Homes, Neighborhoods and Cities.* Cambridge, Mass.: MIT Press, 1981.

———. *Redesigning the American Dream: The Future of Housing, Work, and Family Life.* New York: W.W. Norton, 1984.

Herdeg, Klaus. *Formal Structure in Indian Architecture.* New York: Rizzoli International Publications, 1990.

———. *Formal Structure in Islamic Architecture of Iran and Turkistan.* New York: Rizzoli International Publications, 1990.

Hertzberger, Herman. *Lessons for Students in Architecture.* Rotterdam: Uitgeverij, 1991.

Hillier, Bill. "Against Enclosure." In *Rehumanizing Housing,* edited by Necdet Teymur, Thomas Markus, and Tom Woolley, 63–88. London: Butterworth, 1988.

Hillier, Bill, and Julienne Hanson. *The Social Logic of Space.* Cambridge, England: Cambridge University Press, 1984.

Hillier, Bill, Julienne Hanson, T. Grajewski, and J. Xu. "Natural Movement: Or, Configuration and Attraction in Urban Pedestrian Movement." *Environment and Planning B: Planning and Design* 20 (1993): 29–66.

Historic American Buildings Survey. *The Horatio West Court Apartments.* Survey No. CAL 1930. Washington, D.C.: U.S. National Park Service, 1968.

Howard, Ebenezer. *Garden Cities of Tomorrow.* London: Faber and Faber, 1945.

Jackson, John Brinckerhott. *The Necessity for Ruins and Other Topics.* Amherst: University of Massachusetts Press, 1980.

Jackson, Kenneth. *The Crabgrass Frontier: The Suburbanization of the United States.* New York: Oxford University Press, 1985.

Jacobs, Jane. *The Death and Life of Great American Cities.* New York: Random House, 1961.

Jensen, David. *Community Applications of Density, Design and Cost.* Washington, D.C.: National Association of Home Builders, 1983.

———. *Community Design Guidelines: Responding to a Changing Market.* Washington, D.C.: National Association of Home Builders, 1984.

Jensen, David, and HOH Associates. *Zero Lot Line Housing.* Washington, D.C.: Urban Land Institute, 1981.

Johnson, Matthew. *Housing Culture: Traditional Architecture in an English Landscape.* Washington, D.C.: Smithsonian Institution Press, 1993.

Katz, Peter, ed. *The New Urbanism: Toward an Architecture of Community.* New York: McGraw-Hill, 1994.

Keats, John. *The Crack in the Picture Window.* Boston: Houghton Mifflin, 1956.

Kelbaugh, Douglas, ed. *The Pedestrian Pocket Book: A New Suburban Design Strategy.* New York: Princeton Architectural Press, 1989.

Kelly, Barbara. *Expanding the American Dream: Building and Rebuilding Levittown.* Albany: State University of New York Press, 1993.

Kent, Susan. *Analyzing Activity Areas: An Ethnoarchaeological Study of the Use of Space.* Albuquerque: University of New Mexico Press, 1984.

———, ed. *Method and Theory for Activity Area Research: An Ethno-*

archaeological Approach. New York: Columbia University Press, 1987.

King, Anthony. *The Bungalow: The Production of a Global Culture*. London: Butterworth, 1984.

Knowles, Ralph. "For Those Who Spend Time in a Place." *Places* 8 (Fall 1992): 42–43.

Kostof, Spiro. *America by Design*. New York: Oxford University Press, 1987.

Krieger, Alex, ed. *Andres Duany and Elizabeth Plater-Zyberk: Towns and Town-Making Principles*. New York: Rizzoli International Publications, 1991.

Langdon, Philip. *American Houses*. New York: Stewart, Tabori, and Chang, 1987.

Lavin, Marjorie. "Boundaries in the Built Environment." *Man-Environment Systems* 11 (1981): 195–206.

Lawrence, Roderick J. "Transition Spaces and Dwelling Design." *Journal of Architecture and Planning Research* 1 (1984): 261–271.

———. *Housing, Dwellings and Homes: Design Theory, Research and Practice*. Chichester, England: John Wiley and Sons, 1987.

Lynch, Kevin. *Image of the City*. Cambridge, Mass.: MIT Press, 1960.

———. *What Time Is This Place?* Cambridge, Mass.: MIT Press, 1972.

———. *A Theory of Good City Form*. Cambridge, Mass.: MIT Press, 1981.

MacCormac, Richard C. "The Anatomy of Wright's Aesthetic." In *Writings on Wright*, edited by H. Allen Brooks, 161–188. Cambridge, Mass.: MIT Press, 1981.

March, Lionel. "An Architect in Search of Democracy: Broadacre City." In *Writings on Wright*, edited by H. Allen Brooks, 195–206. Cambridge, Mass.: MIT Press, 1981.

Marcus, Clare C., and Wendy Sarkissian. *Housing as If People Mattered: Site Design Guidelines for Medium-Density Housing*. Berkeley: University of California Press, 1986.

McCoy, Esther. *Five California Architects*. New York: Praeger, 1975.

———. *Case Study Houses, 1945–1962*. Los Angeles: Hennessey and Ingalls, 1977.

Midwest Plan Service. *House Planning Handbook*, 2d ed. Ames: Midwest Plan Service, Iowa State University, 1988.

Moe, Richard, and Carter Wilkie. *Changing Places: Rebuilding Community in the Age of Sprawl.* New York: Henry Holt, 1997.

Moore, Charles, Gerald Allen, and Donlyn Lyndon. *The Place of Houses.* New York: Holt, Rinehart and Winston, 1974.

Moudon, Anne Vernez. *Built for Change: Neighborhood Architecture in San Francisco.* Cambridge, Mass.: MIT Press, 1986.

———. "A Catholic Approach to Organizing What Urban Designers Should Know." *Journal of Planning Literature* 6 (1992): 331–349.

———. "The Evolution of Twentieth-Century Residential Forms: An American Case Study." In *Urban Landscapes: International Perspectives*, edited by Jeremy Whitehand, 170–206. London: Routledge, 1992.

———. "Getting to Know the Built Landscape: Typomorphology." In *Ordering Space: Types in Architecture and Design*, edited by Karen A. Franck and Lynda H. Schneekloth. New York: Van Nostrand Reinhold, 1994.

———. "Teaching Urban Form." *Journal of Planning Education and Research* 14 (1995): 123–133.

———. "Urban Morphology as an Emerging Interdisciplinary Field." *Urban Morphology: Journal of the International Seminar on Urban Form* 1 (1997): 3–10.

Moule, Elizabeth, and Stefanos Polyzoides. "The Street, the Block and the Building." In *The New Urbanism: Toward an Architecture of Community*, edited by Peter Katz, xxi–xxiv. New York: McGraw-Hill, 1994.

Mumford, Lewis. *The City in History: Its Origins, Its Transformations, and Its Prospects.* New York: Harcourt, Brace and World, 1961.

Muratori, Saverio. *Studi per una operante storia urbana di Venezia.* Rome: Istituto Poligrafico dello Stato P.V., 1959.

Norberg-Schulz, Christian. *Intentions in Architecture.* Cambridge, Mass.: MIT Press, 1965.

———. *Existence, Space and Architecture.* New York: Praeger, 1971.

———. *Genius Loci: Towards a Phenomenology of Architecture.* New York: Rizzoli International Publications, 1980.

———. *The Concept of Dwelling: On the Way to Figurative Architecture.* New York: Electa/Rizzoli International Publications, 1985.

Oliver, Paul. *Dwellings: The House across the World.* Austin: University of Texas Press, 1987.

Owens, Mitchell. "Building Small, Thinking Big." *New York Times*, July 21, 1994, B1.

Pader, Ellen J. "Spatiality and Social Change: Domestic Space Use in Mexico and the United States." *American Ethnologist* 20 (1993): 114–136.

Palen, J. John. *The Suburbs.* New York: McGraw-Hill, 1995.

Pallasmaa, Juhani. "Identity, Intimacy and Domicile: Notes of the Phenomenology of Home." In *The Home: Words, Interpretations, Meanings and Environment,* edited by David N. Benjamin. Aldershot, England: Avebury, 1995.

Pfeiffer, Bruce B. *Frank Lloyd Wright Drawings: Masterworks from the Frank Lloyd Wright Archives.* New York: Harry N. Abrams, 1990.

Pikusa, Stefan. "Designing for Functional Adaptation: A Lesson from History." *Architecture Australia* 72 (1983): 62–67.

Ponce, Mary H. *Hoyt Street: An Autobiography.* Albuquerque: University of New Mexico Press, 1993.

Poston, Jonathan, and the Historical Charleston Foundation. *The Building of Charleston: A Guide to the City's Architecture.* Columbia: University of South Carolina Press, 1997.

Proshansky, Harold M., William Ittelson, and Leanne Rivlin, eds. *Environmental Psychology: Man and His Physical Setting.* New York: Holt, Rinehart and Winston, 1970.

Rapoport, Amos. *House Form and Culture.* Englewood Cliffs, N.J.: Prentice-Hall, 1969.

———. "Foreword." In *Housing, Culture, and Design: A Comparative Perspective,* edited by Setha Low and Erve Chambers, xi–xii. Philadelphia: University of Pennsylvania Press, 1989.

———. *Cross-Cultural Studies and Urban Form.* College Park: Urban Studies and Planning Program, University of Maryland, 1993.

Reeve, Agnesa. *From Hacienda to Bungalow: Northern New Mexico Houses, 1850–1912.* Albuquerque: University of New Mexico Press, 1988.

Richardson, Walter. "Designing High Density Single Family Housing: Variation on the Zero Lot Line Theme." *Urban Land* 47 (February 1988): 15–20.

Rosenberg, Dick, Douglas P. Wheeler, Larry Orman, and Daniel M. Leibsohn. *Beyond Sprawl: New Patterns of Growth to Fit the New California.* San Francisco: Bank of America, California Resources

Agency, Greenbelt Alliance, and Low Income Housing Fund, 1995.

Rowe, Colin, and Robert Slutzky. *Transparency*. Boston: Birkhäuser, 1997.

Rowe, Peter G. *Design Thinking*. Cambridge, Mass.: MIT Press, 1987.

———. *Making a Middle Landscape*. Cambridge, Mass.: MIT Press, 1991.

Rowe, Peter, and John Desmond. *The Shape and Appearance of the Modern American Single-Family House*. Cambridge, Mass.: Joint Center for Housing Studies of MIT and Harvard University, 1986.

Rybczynski, Witold. "Should Suburbs Be Designed?" *Atlantic* 269 (1992): 109–112.

Sanborn Map Company, Special Services Division. *Sanborn Services for City and Regional Planners*. Chicago: Sanborn Map Company, 1957.

Sarnitz, August, ed. *R. M. Schindler, Architect: 1887–1953*. New York: Rizzoli International Publications, 1988.

Schaffer, Daniel. *Garden Cities for America: The Radburn Experience*. Philadelphia: Temple University Press, 1982.

Sherman, Roger, ed. *Re: American Dream—Six Urban Housing Prototypes for Los Angeles*. New York: Princeton Architectural Press, 1995.

Sherwood, Roger. *Modern Housing Prototypes*. Cambridge, Mass.: Harvard University Press, 1978.

Short, James, ed. *The Social Fabric of the Metropolis: Contributions of the Chicago School of Urban Sociology*. Chicago: University of Chicago Press, 1971.

Sitte, Camillo. *The Art of Building Cities: City Building According to Its Artistic Fundamentals*. New York: Reinhold, 1945.

Smithson, Alison, ed. *Team 10 Primer*. Cambridge, Mass.: MIT Press, 1968.

Solomon, Daniel. "Life on the Edge: Toward a New Suburbia." *Architectural Record* 184 (November 1988): 63–67.

———. *ReBuilding*. New York: Princeton Architectural Press, 1992.

Sorkin, Michael. "Introduction: Variations on a Theme Park." In *Variations on a Theme Park: The New American City and the End of Public Space*, edited by Michael Sorkin. New York: Hill and Wang, 1992.

Stein, Clarence S. *Toward New Towns for America*. 6th ed. Cambridge, Mass.: MIT Press, 1978.

Stoner, Jill. "The Party Wall as the Architecture of Sharing." In *New Households, New Housing*, edited by Karen A. Franck and Sherry Ahrentzen. New York: Van Nostrand Reinhold, 1994.

Takaki, Ronald. *A Different Mirror: A History of Multicultural America*. Boston: Little, Brown, 1993.

Talcott, Charles, Donald Hepler, and Paul Wallach. *Home Planners' Guide to Residential Design*. New York: McGraw-Hill, 1986.

Tarpoff, Anet, and Pat Talbert. "A House Is Just a Box." *Hills Publication*, real estate section, January 11, 1996.

Taylor, C. Stanley. "Efficiency Planning and Equipment." *Architectural Forum* 41 (1924): 682–687.

Teymur, Necdet, Thomas Markus, and Tom Woolley, eds. *Rehumanizing Housing*. London: Butterworth, 1988.

Thernstrom, Stephan, ed. *Harvard Encyclopedia of American Ethnic Groups*. Cambridge, Mass.: Belknap Press, 1980.

Trancik, Roger. *Finding Lost Space: Theories of Urban Design*. New York: Van Nostrand Reinhold, 1986.

"Up from the Potato Fields." *Time*, July 3, 1950, 67–72.

Vance, James E., Jr. *The Continuing City: Urban Morphology in Western Civilization*. Baltimore: Johns Hopkins University Press, 1990.

Venturi, Robert. "Contradictory Levels Continued: The Double-Functioning Element." In *Complexity and Contradiction in Architecture*. New York: Museum of Modern Art, 1977.

Vickery, Robert L. *Anthrophysical Form: Two Families and Their Neighborhood Environments*. Charlottesville: University Press of Virginia, 1972.

Wachs, Martin, and Margaret Crawford, eds. *The Car and the City: The Automobile, the Built Environment and Daily Urban Life*. Ann Arbor: University of Michigan Press, 1992.

Waters, Mary C. *Ethnic Options: Choosing Identities in America*. Berkeley: University of California Press, 1990.

Wattel, Harold. "Levittown: A Suburban Community." In *The Suburban Community*, edited by William M. Dobriner. New York: G. P. Putnam's Sons, 1958.

Wentling, James. "Technics: Small Lot Housing Typology." *Progressive Architecture* 6 (1991): 45–49.

————. *Designing a Place Called Home.* New York: Chapman and Hall, 1995.

Wentling, James, and Lloyd Bookout, eds. *Density by Design.* Washington, D.C.: Urban Land Institute, 1988.

Whitehand, J. W. R., ed. *The Urban Landscape: Historical Development and Management. Papers by M. R. G. Conzen.* London: Academic Press, 1981.

Whyte, William. *The Organization Man.* Garden City, N.J.: Doubleday Anchor, 1956.

Wilson, Christopher. "When a Room Is the Hall." *Mass: Journal of the School of Architecture and Planning, University of New Mexico* 2 (Summer 1984): 17–23.

Wright, Frank Lloyd. *The Living City.* New York: Bramhall House, 1958.

Wright, Gwendolyn. *Moralism and the Model Home: Domestic Architecture and Cultural Conflict in Chicago, 1873–1913.* Chicago: University of Chicago Press, 1980.

————. *Building the Dream: A Social History of Housing in America.* Cambridge, Mass.: MIT Press, 1981.

illustration credits

Except as noted below, all photographs and illustrations are by the author.

Figure 2: "Tav. II—Quartiere di S. Zulian—Situazione Attuale," by Saverio Muratori. From Saverio Muratori, *Studi per una operante storia urbana di Venezia* (Rome: Istituto Poligrafico dello Stato P.V., 1959).

Figure 3: "The Bottom Level of the Johnson House" and "The Top Level of the Johnson House," by Susan Kent. From Susan Kent, *Analyzing Activity Areas: An Ethnoarchaeological Study of the Use of Space* (Albuquerque: University of New Mexico Press, 1984), 109. Reprinted by permission of Susan Kent.

Figure 5: "Sub-Variations in the Twin Support System." Drawing from N. John Habraken, J. T. Boekholt, P. Dinjens, and A. P. Thijssen, *Variations: The Systematic Design of Supports* (Cambridge, Mass.: Laboratory of Architecture and Planning, MIT, 1976), 143. Reprinted by courtesy of the authors.

Figure 6: Axial map of Barnsbury. From Bill Hillier and Julienne Hanson, *The Social Logic of Space* (Cambridge, England: Cambridge University Press, 1984), 125, fig. 63. Reprinted with the permission of Cambridge University Press.

Figure 7: "The Exterior of the Husser House," designed by Frank Lloyd Wright; drawing by Richard C. MacCormac. From Richard C. MacCormac, "The Anatomy of Wright's Aesthetic," in *Writings on Wright*, H. Allen Brooks, ed. (Cambridge, Mass.: MIT Press, 1981), 170.

Figures 8 and 45: "Area of Avenue Victor-Hugo. Engineering Structure," by Stanford Anderson. From Stanford Anderson, "Studies toward an Ecological Model of the Urban Environment," in *On Streets*, Stanford Anderson, ed. (Cambridge, Mass.: MIT Press, 1978), 292, fig. 29.

Figure 15: Quadruple block plan, by Frank Lloyd Wright. From Yukio Futagawa and B. Pfeiffer, eds., *Frank Lloyd Wright Monographs 1902–1906* (Tokyo: A. D. A. Edita, 1987), 66, fig. 117, Block Plan B. The drawings of Frank Lloyd Wright are copyright © 1987, 2001 The Frank Lloyd Wright Foundation, Scottsdale, AZ.

Figure 18: "Plan of Residential Districts Dated November 1929," by Clarence S. Stein. From Clarence S. Stein, *Toward New Towns for America*, 6th ed. (Cambridge, Mass.: MIT Press, 1978), 43, fig. 21.

Figure 21: Aerial photo of Levittown in 1957, by Joseph Scherschel/*Life*. Courtesy of TimePix.

Figure 22: "Theoretical Study of a Superblock Dated January 17, 1928," by Clarence S. Stein. From Clarence S. Stein, *Toward New Towns for America*, 6th ed. (Cambridge, Mass.: MIT Press, 1978), 38, fig. 17.

Figure 34: Built-unbuilt plan of a piazza in Lucca, by Camillo Sitte. From Camillo Sitte, *The Art of Building Cities: City Building According to Its Artistic Fundamentals* (New York: Reinhold, 1945).

Figure 35: Plan of Schilders area, The Hague, by H. Reyenga. From N. John Habraken, *SAR '73: The Methodical Formulations of Agreements Concerning the Direct Dwelling Environment* (Eindhoven, the Netherlands: Stichting Architekten Research, 1973), 2.4. Courtesy of SAR.

Figure 36: "Houston, Texas—August, 1885—Section 12," by the Sanborn Map Company. Copyright 1885 The Sanborn Map Company, The Sanborn Library, LLC. All Rights Reserved. This Sanborn® Map has been reproduced with written permission from The Sanborn Library, LLC. All further reproductions are prohibited without prior written permission from The Sanborn Library, LLC.

Figures 37a, 37b, 37c: "The San Francisco Peninsula," "Alamo Square 1931," and "Typology of House Forms and Lots—Wide and Narrow Single Lots," by Anne Vernez Moudon. From Anne Vernez Moudon, *Built for Change: Neighborhood Architecture in San Francisco* (Cambridge, Mass.: MIT Press, 1986), 2, fig. 1.3; 17, fig. 1.17; 61, fig. 2.13. Courtesy of Anne Vernez Moudon.

Figures 38a, 38b, 38c, 38d: "Locality Circulation Plan," "Locality Segment Plan," "Dwelling Group," and "Typical Dwelling," by Horacio Caminos et al. From Horacio Caminos, John Turner, and John Steffian, *Urban Dwelling Environments: An Elementary Survey of Settlements for the Study of Design Determinants* (Cambridge, Mass.: MIT Press, 1969), 108, 110, 112, 114.

Figure 42: Rome in 1748, by Giambattista Nolli, from his *Pianta Grande di Roma*.

Figure 43: "Different Perceptions of the Maidan," by Klaus Herdeg. From Klaus Herdeg, *Formal Structure in Islamic Architecture of Iran and Turkistan* (New York: Rizzoli International Publications, 1990), 19. Courtesy Rizzoli International Publications, New York.

Figure 44: "Tav. VII—Quartiere di S. Cangiano—S. Maria Nova—Situazione Attuale," by Saverio Muratori. From Saverio Muratori, *Studi per una operante storia urbana di Venezia* (Rome: Istituto Poligrafico dello Stato P.V., 1959).

Figure 94: "Different Area Relationships." From Charles Talcott, Donald Hepler, and Paul Wallach, *Home Planners' Guide to Residential Design* (New York: McGraw-Hill, 1986), 67, fig. 4–2. Reproduced with permission of The McGraw-Hill Companies.

Figure 96: "Plan of Development at Radburn Completed by 1930," by Clarence S. Stein. From Clarence S. Stein, *Toward New Towns for America*, 6th ed. (Cambridge, Mass.: MIT Press, 1978), 49, fig. 26.

Figure 105: "Williamsburg Neighborhood," photograph by Ted Kirk. *Lincoln Journal Star*, Nebraska, September 30, 1995, p. 8A. Reprinted by permission of the *Lincoln Journal Star* newspaper.

Figures 120a, 120b, 120c: Model *a* by Jane Lee, model *b* by Neil Harrigan and Angela Barreda, model *c* by Kari Kimura. All prepared for a class taught by the author at the Department of Architecture, MIT.

Figure 128: "New Homes in Pittsburg Line Up on the Northern Foothills of Mount Diablo," aerial photograph by Karl Mondon. *Contra Costa Times*, March 26, 1999, p. B1. Reprinted by permission of the Contra Costa Newspapers Inc.

Figure 137: "Alley at Pueblo Ribera," photograph by Brent Hinrichs. Reprinted by permission of Brent Hinrichs.

Figure 142: Inhabitation information for southwestern house provided by E.E. Fava, architect, of Charleston, South Carolina.

index

Page numbers in italics indicate figures: e.g., *74fig.67* indicates figure 67 on page 74.

DESIGNER: SEVENTEENTH STREET STUDIOS
COMPOSITOR: SEVENTEENTH STREET STUDIOS
TEXT: ELECTRA LH
DISPLAY: FRUTIGER
PRINTER: EDWARDS BROTHERS, INC.
BINDER: EDWARDS BROTHERS, INC.